A GATHERING
OF STRANGERS

A GATHERING OF STRANGERS

Understanding the Life of Your Church

Revised and Updated Edition

by

ROBERT C. WORLEY

THE WESTMINSTER PRESS
Philadelphia

Book Design by Alice Derr

First edition

Published by The Westminster Press®
Philadelphia, Pennsylvania

PRINTED IN THE UNITED STATES OF AMERICA
9 8 7 6 5 4 3 2 1

Library of Congress Cataloging in Publication Data

Worley, Robert C.
A gathering of strangers.

Includes bibliographical references.
1. Church. 2. Theology, Practical. I. Title.
BV600.2.W66 1983   250   83-12343
ISBN 0-664-24488-2 (pbk.)

To my sons
Robert S. and Peter

CONTENTS

LIST OF FIGURES

LIST OF EXERCISES

PREFACE
TO REVISED AND UPDATED EDITION

The original edition of this book has been used as a resource for governing boards and adult study groups who have desired to understand their own church better, and to be more effective Christian leaders. Seminary faculty have used the book as a text in both Master of Divinity and Doctor of Ministry programs. This Revised and Updated Edition has been altered to reflect these uses of the book. Several sections, particularly the sections on "structure" and "power," have been strengthened. New material has been cited and the major ideas have been dealt with in a more substantial manner. Overall, the major effort has been to help the reader to see the relationship between the church as social organization and the theology of the church.

Since the first edition was written, Old Testament scholars have confirmed, in their own ways, the relationship between social organization and the religion of Israel. Walter Brueggemann in "Trajectories in Old Testament Literature and the Sociology of Ancient Israel," *Journal of Biblical Literature*, Vol. 98, No. 2 (1979), maintains that Israel experimented socially by creating a form of social life based on a vision of the meaning of the covenant-treaty. Norman Gottwald in *The Tribes of Yahweh* (Orbis Books, 1979) adds yet another insight that is important to the themes of this book. All ideas, including religious ideas, have social contexts. The environmental contexts are of consequence for both our theological ideas and our social organization. "For early Israel," he states, "the interest is the contrast between an egalitarian view of reality and an hierarchic view of reality, each of which comes to expression and is indirectly reinforced in a notion of God and each of which is embodied and directly enforced in a form of sociopolitical organization" (p. 912). George Mendenhall states what appears to be the new understanding of Old Testament scholars: "Religious faith is thus intimately bound up with social organization in the Bible" (*The Tenth Generation,* p. 183; Johns Hopkins University Press, 1973).

It is important for the reader to ask: How is Christian faith bound to the forms of social organization which are called church today? What are the conditions in the church within which and against which thought takes form? What are various groups thinking in the church because of the conditions that exist in the sanctuary, governing board and committee meetings, church school classes, and in the church as a whole expressive entity? What notions of God, church, Spirit, human being, and world are embedded in these powerful living entities?

Readers are urged to understand Christian faith as something more and other than a set of religious ideas for individuals to believe. Christian faith, as the faith of ancient Israel, emerged and transformed ordinary life, even the religious forms of life. You are invited to see, experience, and think about life in the church and world and engage in a social experiment in this time to create a social organization that embodies a profound and worthy understanding of God, Spirit, Christ, person, and church.

INTRODUCTION

"The body of Christ," "the New Israel," "a holy nation," and a host of other phrases were used by New Testament writers to symbolize the early gatherings of Christians. These evoke few concrete images in our minds today. An urban, complex, organizational world does not recapture easily the rich meanings inherent in the terms used by early Christians.

This book is about the church and its ministry today. Words and thought forms drawn from contemporary life are used to open our eyes and minds to see what really exists today, and how what exists relates to what God is doing in the church and the world. The passions of persons, the complexities of groups, the forms of power and their use in congregational life, and the dynamic influence of the environment surrounding a congregation are missed as we use words from the past to inform the present. The major point of the book is that the church is a gathering of strangers. The strangers are gathered in complex relationships that beg attention and reflection.

The usual order of writing a book of this type is to begin with explicit theological statements and Biblical quotations in order to legitimatize what follows. The order is reversed in this book. The author desires the material presented in the early chapters to stand on its own. It is legitimate information which enriches and informs the task of thinking as Christians about the church. The use of contemporary language and thought forms should provide the reader with images that make the task of thinking as Christians more pointed and fruitful.

Behind the writing of this book is a gnawing question: Is it possible for the church to be Christian? Behind the question lies the assumption that the church is more than the religious words uttered in sermons, prayers, hymns, and litanies. The essence of the church is not found in its language, but in its being the people among whom God reigns. As the prophets declared to Israel prior to the new covenant, God's reign is not confined to worship services. God reigns in the everyday life of the people, including congregational life. The early chapters are provided to enable Christians to have a more accurate picture of the church we experience as the context for reflection as Christians about the church and ministry.

The danger in using thought forms and categories from the present moment is that these may distort the nature of Christian faith. There is always risk involved in attempting to discern what God is up to among the people. Christians in every age have taken the risk, and we have noted their faithfulness and distortions in our histories. New tools for symbolizing the meaning of Christian faith, and making its meaning poignant are present when contemporary sources are used. The dangers are certainly no greater than those of absolutizing the words and our interpretations of them from any previous century.

Faith, trust, and loyalty to God requires us to live in the present, using contemporary tools as well as the traditional language and inherited forms of thought, to think about the church and ministry. The book is written in a sequence intended to facilitate reflection upon contemporary issues as well as our inheritance as we seek to be truthful to God, other persons, and ourselves.

McCormick Theological Seminary is a good place to work. Faculty members are encouraged to think about the church and ministry from different perspectives. They are given freedom by the Board of Directors and the Administration to live out commitments as scholars and teachers for the church. I am grateful for this as well as the generous sabbatical leave policy which made the writing of this book possible.

Several colleagues on the faculty have provided encouragement as they have worked from their own perspective on the church and ministry. I am grateful particularly to Jack L. Stotts, president of McCormick, George Magnuson, John Burkhart, Thomas Parker, and Robert Evans. The Ethics and Theology departments continually raise helpful questions and offer positive directions. Phyllis Koehnline and Patti Houck Sprenkle have my gratitude for their editorial assistance.

A GATHERING
OF STRANGERS

CHAPTER 1

Toward a New Perspective
on the Church

This book is written to provide the church with a tool that will enable persons in the church to see better what is going on in the congregational life. What is happening to members, old and new? What is grasping clergy and lay leadership from all sides? What is the quality and character of ministry and mission in the congregation? What is the dynamism and complexity of an ordinary congregation?

It is a tool not only to *see* better what is but also to *say* what is. It aims to help church members talk about themselves and congregational life and reflect together as Christ's people about what is seen and said. Seeing, talking, and thinking about what is seen is important in order to perceive even more than what would ordinarily be visible. Depth of perception comes when others help us to see. Reflecting together is crucial to develop common perceptions, motivations, and commitments to create something even better.

The commitment to create something better, or to affirm what is, hinges on accurately seeing what is and creating a vision of what might be. In this instance, the word "better" refers to the possibility that the church might be more Christlike—that commitments which have to do with God's reconciling work among people, God's acceptance of us, and our acceptance, in turn, of people, might be more profoundly and appropriately expressed in the life of a congregation.

The first step is to see *what is*. All church members do not see a congregation with the same confidence that Christian faith is being expressed. All church people do not see the same things when they look at the congregation.

Moreover, each person has a point of view for seeing the church which is largely unexpressed and unexamined. This perspective contains assumptions about the purposes of the church. It includes specific goals and objectives, structure, leadership, style, relationships to surrounding environments, and rules and procedures for doing the church's work. Most persons have not examined their perspectives. Little is known about why they see the church as they do. Since the church is a religious institution, assumptions about it are not examined. The purpose and nature of schools, work organizations, and government may be questioned and alternative perspectives proposed. But rarely in the church dare we imagine that a better perspective might be found.

The climate that prevails in the church frequently prohibits this search for a more profound and helpful view of the congregation. Church leaders still attempt to rule wisely using the patterns, style, and tools of previous generations in a society that has long since developed other ways of seeing human organizations. They mistakenly assume that ancient practices, prevalent in society and adopted by the church are uniquely Presbyterian, Lutheran, or Episcopalian. However, there is nothing uniquely Christian about older cultural perspectives on persons, the nature of the church, or the purpose of the church in society—perspectives that have been embedded in leadership styles, structures, and processes of congregations and other types of church organizations. In feudal society, for example, the church was one of the two or three dominant institutions (and much of the time it was impossible to distinguish between them). Ways of doing things, established in a particular cultural setting, have an impressive power to persist long after the situation has changed.

Throughout the centuries theologians have engaged in multiple and fascinating attempts to reform the word pictures of Christian faith. New confessions of faith and countless controversies have been recorded as evidence that someone has paid attention to the *words* of Christianity. Much less attention has been given to other expressions of faith: structure, decision-making and political processes, human relations in the church, rules and procedures that govern persons, the quality and character of the purposes of congregations in real life. Historians have discovered ample evidence that the medieval church was the creation of monarchs, lords, barons, and clergy as they struggled with one another for power and authority. The church was an instrument of power in the struggle. An educated clergy in an uneducated society employed theological rationales for their various actions. Moreover, the clergy owned land. There was a time when over 50 percent of the land of Scotland was in one way or another possessed by the church. In the power struggle between the established church and its reformers, embryonic structures, processes, leadership styles, and purposes of the church arose.[1] Embedded within these forms and patterns are perspectives on persons, conceptions of the nature and purpose of the church in society, leadership styles, and mechanisms for maintaining control and "purity" of the church.

Many church people—clergy and laity—are still victimized by these perspectives. The unexamined, hidden assumptions and the attitudes that accompany them are extremely powerful in human life. Perspectives of persons are not consciously constructed. They are learned in families, churches, schools, and other human organizations. Perspectives are powerful because they determine how a person comes to see what is going on in an organization. Therefore individuals are limited by their framework for seeing what is happening.

Perspective influences greatly not only what is seen but also what is not seen. For example, if one's perspective holds that the congregation is an organization that exists primarily for the eleven o'clock hour on Sunday morning, and particularly for the preaching at that hour, then that person cannot understand the profound dynamics created by persons who see the church in different ways. If persons with other perspectives are noticed at all, they are often seen as misinformed, or troublesome, or discontented. These persons with different perspectives may have pronounced effects on church behavior, but tools are lacking for seeing, understanding, and acting more appropriately within a congregation in which there are multiple perspectives. Perspectives can blind persons as well as open up new phenomena for observation and reflection.

The perspectives through which persons see reality influence the prescriptions and solutions that are created in order to respond to what is assumed to be there. Persons actively construct their view of reality out of the material available to them, which their perspective makes available. Persons then create programs, public relations efforts, sermons, speeches, prayers, and coalitions of like-minded persons on the basis of the world picture which they have created. The picture may be good or bad, accurate or inaccurate, depending upon the adequacy of the perspective with which the situation is evaluated.

Perspectives of what is there in a congregation, what is happening and why it is happening, determine to a great extent the role of clergy, leaders, and members. Persons respond to what they see by using the tools, skills, and ideas which they think are appropriate to that view. They respond with these resources in traditional roles. Limited or inadequate perspectives may bring forth erroneous responses in the use of resources, and in the choice of roles. When there is turbulence in the world outside of persons, a group or organization, and persons have inadequate perspectives on that world, problems of knowing who one is in the unmanageable environment result. Partial perspectives do not allow persons to organize and mobilize their personal resources or to alter their ways of behaving to ones that might be more effective and appropriate.

This book is written in an attempt to provide a different perspective on the church, one that enables clergy and laity to understand how it functions, so that congregational life is a more appropriate and effective expression of Christian faith. New tools and ideas are provided for viewing congregational life. The intent is to provide a perspective and resources that will help persons understand not only the congregation but themselves as actors in the drama of creative congregational life. With such a perspective, it is hoped that the reforming process of congregations will continue so that the artifacts of the future will bear witness not only to our words but also to the reformation of everyday congregational life and of persons in the church.

Exercises have been provided to facilitate seeing what is going on in a congregation. The hope is that groups will use such exercises, examine the content of the figures and diagrams with a thoughtfulness that will lead them beyond mere dissatisfaction and criticism to the creation of conditions in a congregation which are more expressive of Christian faith. Readers should feel free to change the language and alter the design of an exercise so that it is most helpful to them. Group study and reflection is strongly encouraged. Different perspectives about a congregation exist and can be shared in groups. Reflection is sharper and more substantive when the ideas of several persons are put forth and persons search together for those goals and organizational arrangements which are the products of active moral discernment.

CHAPTER 2

Getting Hold of Oneself

James Luther Adams comments on the relationship between Christian faith and human institutions: "It must be recognized, however, that institutionalization has an ambiguous character. It may give order to social existence, but it may also impose intolerable fetters."[2] Rarely do we examine the relationship between Christian faith and the institutionalized expressions and consequences of that faith. Since Christian faith has everything to do with persons, groups, and the church, it is essential that church leaders examine the current consequences of faith as expressed in the life of the church today. Christian faith is in a dynamic relationship to the forms in which that faith is expressed. The institutional forms created by church persons are complex, powerful expressions of a person's or group's understanding of faith. In an important sense, the institutional forms are one meaning of the faith.

The institutional forms with their embedded meanings of Christian faith define and shape persons and groups. Institutional forms with their inherent meanings establish or disestablish persons and groups. It is impossible for some church members to "get hold of themselves," to know themselves as gifted, worthy, powerful, contributing, active members of some churches. The forms, and perhaps the faith as expressed in that church, identify them otherwise.

Our words—pastor, minister, layman, laywoman, churchman, churchwoman—have a variety of negative and positive meanings. There is ambiguity as to what behaviors, attitudes, and interests are appropriate for both laity and clergy. There is certainly a lack of clarity and consistency about what it means to be a seminary student. There are no common conceptions of piety, of commitment, and of attitudes appropriate for students contemplating professional ministry. Formerly the Orders within Roman Catholicism had their own distinguishing characteristics: particular acts of piety, ritual, interests, and attitudes toward self, church, and world. The decline of the Orders in the present time is only a bit of evidence of the increasing confusion as to what is meant by a "church person."

In earlier days there were definitions of behaviors, attitudes, and interests that were generally accepted as appropriate for persons with different kinds of membership, status, and responsibilities in the church. These definitions were creations of men and women and were more or less fitting to a given social world of the time. Even then, the fit of a given definition depended on the perspective of the person viewing and on the conditions surrounding the church. For example, the manner of preaching and teaching, the style of leadership, and the expected pious acts have varied with the congregation, community, denomination, and nation. Nevertheless, there were definitions, more or less recognized and accepted, that give a functioning unity to the churches.

It is no longer so in our own day. Our current lack of common definitions has led to frustration, bitterness, and even withdrawal from the church by both clergy and laity. The absence of commonly accepted definitions means that persons do not feel they have a place, do not know who they are in the congregation. It means they are not established as persons in the church. In the turbulence of contemporary congregational life diverse definitions of behavior, attitudes, and interests exist. Church members have great difficulty dealing with this diversity. In the midst of competing and conflicting ideas and expectations, they suffer an identity crisis.

The phrase "identity crisis" has been used in many ways. Here it is used as originally suggested by Erik Erickson. In his study of disturbed adolescent boys he observed that in late adolescence there is a process of evaluating the relationships between an individual's image of himself and his image of life outside the self. It is "the conscious attempt of the growing human being, for the first time, to formulate *rules* or *patterns* of the relation between a self-image and an image of the world outside the self."[3]

When institutions and societies are undergoing rapid change, it is difficult to devise the rules and patterns necessary for knowing and establishing who one is in a particular setting. With diverse expectations and definitions in an institution such as the church, it is difficult to be a minister or a pastor. One faces diverse expectations from those served, and in addition one's own self-image is often confused. Nor is it easy to be a leader, layman, or laywoman. Church members have not learned how to deal with the diversity of expectations and definitions that exist in that piece of a person's social world, the church. Frequently, attempts to change the church are met with hostility as members resist the destruction of such rules and patterns as they have found to establish themselves as persons.

How "personhood" is formed is not well understood, but increasingly organizations are seen as the primary locus for identity formation. It is in organizations such as the family, church, schools, work, and voluntary associations that persons are formed and re-formed with their own active participation in the process.

The formation of identity is largely the result of both sociological and biological factors. Erich Fromm, in *The Anatomy of Human Destructiveness,* has summarized the arguments against the "instinctivists," who hold that personhood is primarily a product of instinctual drives, organic in nature. Fromm himself sets forth a more complex and more satisfying theory, arguing that his own framework

> frees such passions as the strivings to love, to be free, as well as the drive to destroy, to torture, to control and to submit, from their forced marriage to instincts. Instincts are a purely natural category, while the character-rooted passions are a sociobiological, historical category. Although not directly serving physical survival they are as strong—and often stronger—than instincts. They form the basis for man's interest in life, his enthusiasm, his excitement; they are the stuff from which not only his dreams are made but art, religion, myth, drama—all that makes life worth living. Man cannot live as nothing but an object, as dice thrown out of a cup; he suffers severely when he is reduced to the level of a feeding or propagating machine, even if he has all the security he wants. Man seeks for drama and excitement; when he cannot get satisfaction on a higher level, he creates for himself the drama of destruction.[4]

What Fromm calls "the sociobiological, historical category" is used as a basic concept in this book, particularly as it pertains to the church as a human institution called into existence by God. The church is the location where sociology (persons in groups and

organizational arrangements) and biology (instincts, genes, organic drives and needs) meet. The church consists of real persons
who exist at a given place and time. We have sometimes acted as
though the church were "ahistorical," standing outside history
reflecting in some pure form the intent and meaning of the good
news of God's activity in Jesus Christ. But God alone is the "wholly
Other," not at our disposal, not shaped by human activity. The
church as the living body of God's people is a human institution
touched, manipulated, altered, and transformed by human beings.

We have paid scant attention to what human beings touch, the
church itself. We have scrutinized only rarely the historical forms
of the church: its structure, decision-making, political and communication processes, its rewards and punishments. And we have
largely ignored the consequences of these forms for individuals
(both clergy and lay). Roman Catholic theologians have made the
connections between theology and church life most visible. Prot-
estants have virtually ignored them. But it is sociobiological, historical forms that create human conditions of cynicism, bitterness,
frustration, and crises of identity. The human forms of the church,
not the "wholly Other," God, create ambiguity in our commitment and provide that wealth of reality outside of persons which
often paralyzes and destroys those passions which Christianity has
historically nurtured.

We cannot hold the secular world responsible for the identity
crisis of the church. We in the church are responsible for our own
creations. We create and maintain what we have. If ministers are
immobilized by diversity, or are ambiguous about appropriate
behaviors for themselves in the congregation, or if they are rigid
and unbending in the face of new challenges, we dare not claim
that such conditions are mere defects in their character. Or if
laypersons are apathetic or resistant, or if they form pressure
groups, or simply drop out, we cannot claim that they are the
problem. Few persons, apparently, understand the processes of
institutions, and the power they exert on persons.

It is a common assumption that individuals shape institutions.
Therefore the prescription that is made for every church problem
is to get rid of the troublemaker, be it the minister, an assistant or
associate, a disgruntled layperson, or a group of disgruntled lay
persons. We have not asked how institutions shape persons. We do
not perceive the institution as the source of our difficulties. We do
not think institutionally, but individualistically. For this reason,
when a minister is in trouble or a layperson is seen as a problem,

we locate the problem in the person. It becomes a personality or character problem rather than an institutional one.

This book makes no claim that the source of all problems of individuals is institutional. It is evident, however, that the tendency has been to use individual psychology, psychoanalysis, transactional analysis, etc., to diagnose individual failure. Here the point is made that the character, climate, goals, structure, processes, and other organizational attributes also have a powerful influence, one that until recently has been ignored.

It is clear that institutions are where personal identity is formed. Persons are established or disestablished as persons in human organizations, of which the church is one. For both laity and clergy, understanding the life of the church is essential for getting hold of oneself and one's ministry. Until persons are at one with themselves, they are not free as persons to live out their commitments and passions. Until persons are effective in transforming the church, they can neither get hold of themselves nor engage in ministry where faith commitments lead them.

Since John Calvin wrote the *Institutes of the Christian Religion* in the sixteenth century, much of Protestantism has understood that ministry is engaged in the transformation of culture. Calvin stated that God is sovereign. God reigns over all creation, including all human creations. God is reigning through the transformation of human structures until they embody God's purposes. H. Richard Niebuhr developed the contemporary expression of Calvin's message in his book *Christ and Culture*. Niebuhr expressed his message through the phrase "Christ the transformer of culture." Christ is in the world and among the people, calling them to transform their creations to carry out God's purposes in the world.

Christ's work among people has been that of developing them as human beings in love, justice, dignity, and freedom to do God's work. Christ's work in contemporary language may be described as "identity formation" of persons and groups. Christian faith is involved with forming rules and patterns of the relationship between a member's self-image and his or her image of the world outside the self. It is involved with the development of Christians who perform different functions for Christ's church, clergy and laity, leaders and members.

A significant aspect of ministry is to understand the church's identity-forming processes. Until this is accomplished, persons cannot be involved in the shaping of their own lives, and a large area of the calling of Christians is ignored, namely, to engage in Christ's work of transforming human creations to accomplish God's purposes.

Ministry, therefore, is the creation and re-creation of culture, of institutions including the church, by and for both clergy and laity. Ministry is not just the minister's preaching, teaching, and counseling. It is laypersons and ministers together getting hold of the church (and themselves in the process) and transforming it to embody Christian faith, and, thereby, to create those identity-forming processes in which persons grow in love, justice, beneficence, dignity, and freedom.

CHAPTER 3

Personal and Organizational Goals

Throughout much of the history of the church the ordinary member has been expected to be passive and dependent. Innovation, initiation, and aggressiveness in everyday life were apt to be rewarded with the lash, imprisonment, fines, or even death. Subservience to kings, earls, lords, and church rulers was expected and demanded. Rulers were aggressive, active, innovative. No one expected ordinary persons, inside or outside the church, to be passionate in the pursuit of commitments. Nor were they expected to reflect upon the meaning of events, ideas, or faith for a community, church, or nation. Only leaders did these things. If the Scriptures suggest something different, it indicates how far Christianity has moved from its sources. One has only to read the hymns and prayers of the past several hundred years to see the picture of a passive person resigned to his or her human lot, trusting in God alone for deliverance from the miseries of life.

Today this image of a subservient, passive believer is foreign to us. It is seen only when we visit other cultures and observe feudal patterns that still survive. It is also glimpsed by looking behind such terms as women's liberation, black power, red power, Hispanic power.

Individuals today, inside and outside the church, are active. They are interested in developing their capacities, themselves, and their commitments in effective ways. Our image of personhood is one of becoming, doing, making, and creating.

In his debate with those who have argued that only instincts have intense motivating power, Erich Fromm stated:

If one discards this mechanistic, reductionist viewpoint and starts from a holistic premise, one begins to realize that man's drives must be seen in terms of their function for the life process of the whole organism. Their intensity is not due to specific physiological needs, but to the need of the whole organism to survive—to grow both physically and mentally.

These passions do not become powerful only *after* the more elementary ones have been satisfied. They are at the very root of human existence and not a kind of luxury which we can afford after the normal, "lower" needs have been satisfied. People have committed suicide because of their failure to realize their passions for love, power, fame, revenge. Cases of suicide because of a lack of sexual satisfaction are virtually nonexistent. These noninstinctual passions excite man, fire him on, make life worth living. . . .

The human passions transform man from a mere thing into a hero, into a being that in spite of tremendous handicaps tries to make sense of life. He wants to be his own creator, to transform his state of being unfinished into one with some goal and some purpose, allowing him to achieve some degree of integration.

Man's passions . . . are *"man's attempts to make sense out of life and to experience the optimum of intensity and strength he can (or believes he can) achieve under the given circumstances."* They are his religion, his cult, his ritual, which he has to hide (even from himself) in so far as they are disapproved by his group.[5]

A perspective that attempts to help persons understand the behavior of congregations and other types of organizations must begin with some assumptions about the actors in these organizations. (See Figure 1 for a diagrammatic description of the perspective.) Human beings are characteristically purposeful in their behaviors. The most important aspect of a person is the purposes or goals that lie behind his or her behavior. Most persons are active in the pursuit of their goals, particularly if they realistically expect at some future time to attain them. On the other hand, persons who do not expect to attain their goals tend to be passive and immobilized. Passiveness does not mean lack of goals or purpose. Rather, it is a momentary state from which persons can be aroused if persuaded that their purposes can be achieved. Therefore we can accurately view persons in the church as active, passionate beings with a capacity to activate themselves to express their passions which have sources in Christian faith.

A viewpoint that believes persons are motivated only through instincts, and a "stimulus-response" perspective that believes a carrot and stick are needed to activate persons, are both inadequate. These perspectives simply do not explain the dynamism and complexity of human beings. Purposeful individuals participate in the church. Their participation is directed toward attaining goals that spring from values from theological and ideological commitments, and from their particular and unique understandings of self.

Persons have varying resources to commit to the attainment of their goals in the church. Their directions reflect what has "captured" them through years of listening to preaching, attending church school classes, living in a culture with religious overtones, and participating in peer groups that have attitudes regarding religion. The church therefore has produced persons with goals in the church. These goals may or may not be articulated and examined. That is, persons may not be highly aware of and intentional about the directions they are pursuing. Consequently, an important feature in understanding the behavior of the church is to see how persons act to express themselves, and what goals have captured their commitment.

PERSONAL GOALS

Individuals express their passion in multiple ways. First of all, passions can be seen in personal goals or goals for self. As persons participate in congregations they do have goals for themselves. Election to a governing board, receiving personal recognition for various contributions and activities, being involved in a particular congregational program, experiencing Christianity in a particular form of liturgy, hearing preaching which is personally satisfying, singing in the choir, teaching in the church school, and working in a youth group are some of the ways in which personal goals are attained. They find such experiences meaningful and self-fulfilling.

PERSONAL GOALS FOR THE CHURCH

Secondly, individuals have personal goals for the congregation. Members seek more or less actively to express their commitments and self-understanding in goals for the congregation. If commitments are important to persons, they seek to embed them in

FIGURE 1
A PERSPECTIVE FOR UNDERSTANDING CHURCH ORGANIZATIONS

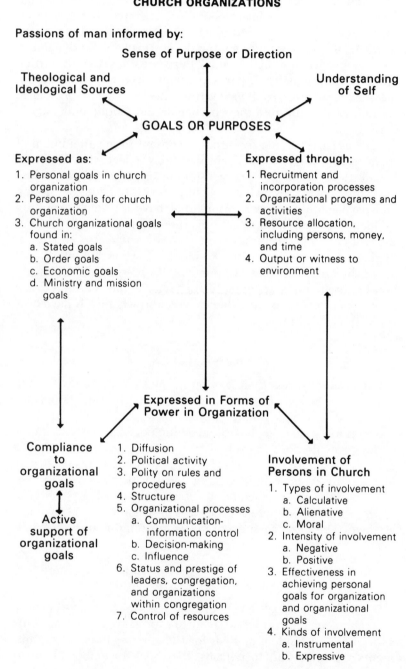

Passions of man informed by:

Sense of Purpose or Direction

Theological and
Ideological Sources

Understanding
of Self

GOALS OR PURPOSES

Expressed as:

1. Personal goals in church
   organization
2. Personal goals for church
   organization
3. Church organizational goals
   found in:
   a. Stated goals
   b. Order goals
   c. Economic goals
   d. Ministry and mission
      goals

Expressed through:

1. Recruitment and
   incorporation processes
2. Organizational programs and
   activities
3. Resource allocation,
   including persons, money,
   and time
4. Output or witness to
   environment

Expressed in Forms of
Power in Organization

Compliance
to
organizational
goals

Active
support of
organizational
goals

1. Diffusion
2. Political activity
3. Polity on rules and
   procedures
4. Structure
5. Organizational processes
   a. Communication-
      information control
   b. Decision-making
   c. Influence
6. Status and prestige of
   leaders, congregation,
   and organizations
   within congregation
7. Control of resources

Involvement of
Persons in Church

1. Types of involvement
   a. Calculative
   b. Alienative
   c. Moral
2. Intensity of involvement
   a. Negative
   b. Positive
3. Effectiveness in
   achieving personal
   goals for organization
   and organizational
   goals
4. Kinds of involvement
   a. Instrumental
   b. Expressive

enduring, significant forms of congregational life. Their desire is to see personal goals for a congregation become congregational goals. The more important one's personal goals become, the greater the desire to see them woven into significant forms of congregational life. Active participation in committees and groups to improve church education, to develop contemporary liturgy for congregational worship, to raise money for an addition to the church, and to establish significant ministries in the community are all ways in which some members seek to implement their personal goals for the congregation. Implementation of these goals always has implications for some part of the congregational structure and for the allocation of congregational resources: time, service, ideas, and money.

All active members have both personal goals and personal goals for a congregation. Most of the tension in the church is due to competition and conflict between persons, including the pastor, who have different personal goals for themselves and for the church.

CONGREGATIONAL GOALS

In addition to personal goals and personal goals for the congregation, the organization itself has goals. These are expressed in processes for recruiting and incorporating new members, in congregational programs and activities, in allocation of resources, and in the visible witness of the church to its members and the community.

There are three types of organizational or congregational goals.

Maintenance goals include the care of property and other assets, church attendance, orderly processes for doing church business, style and content of worship and education, and style of congregational life. These goals are directed toward maintaining the faith and life of the congregation and toward the participation of members in church activities.

Ministry and mission goals may include care of members, programs for the elderly and the young in the church and the community, social action projects, and political involvement in the community. These goals are directed toward expressing Christian faith in witness and service.

Economic goals may include the areas of stewardship, budget development, and efficiency in organizational operations. These goals are directed toward adequate financial support for congregational program and activities.

Organizational goals create opportunities for some persons who see the possibility of personal fulfillment in these goals. Other persons look at existing congregational goals and conclude that either such goals do not belong in the congregation, or there must be a change in the nature and/or priority of goals.

Most persons are committed to a mixture of maintenance, ministry and mission, and economic goals, and there is general consistency in this personal mixture. Goals of all types will tend to be more traditional in some persons and more progressive in others.

A congregation that copes well in its environment will have all three types of goals and persons who are committed to them. The presence of different types of goals in a congregation means that there will be competition for resources. Priority and organizational commitment to the different types of goals will vary because persons value each type differently. Tension is a part of an effective congregation, since it must choose how to allocate its resources among different goals. The goals of persons and personal goals in a congregation are always expressed in relation to current congregational goals. Thus, persons with passion are expressing their hopes and concerns about past, present, and future goals. This makes for a complexity in congregational life which is little understood or appreciated.

Amitai Etzioni, in *A Comparative Analysis of Complex Organizations,* develops a theory of organizational behavior around the concept and modes of compliance.[6] While he has contributed substantially to my theoretical perspective, this book has a different starting point. He is interested primarily in understanding and explaining how leaders and leadership groups in business and industry cause members to accept or comply with their goals. This book, however, starts from a different perspective. We are concerned with people who act in church organizations. They have passion shaped by ideological, theological, and transcendent elements. And they belong to an organization that affects this passion and interprets its sources. Both people and their organization are active. To see passions at work in their positive forms we must consider the tasks designed to achieve the goals of both the persons and the organization. Goals may be explicit and implicit, examined and unexamined, competing and conflicting.

Church organizations are best understood through a perception of persons who have personal goals for themselves, personal goals for the congregation, all in relation to existing congregational goals. Persons are seen at work in the various goal-task areas, i.e.,

Christian education, stewardship, community service, budget and finance, new member recruitment. Each goal-task area is in direct competition for resources with all other goal-task areas. Every congregation has some priority, implicit or explicit, for ranking goals and tasks. How important certain goals and tasks are to leadership groups influences the amount and kind of resources allotted to them.

In each goal-task area there are persons who form a constituent group within the total congregation. These groups are committed in varying degrees to perform the tasks necessary to achieve the goals lodged in their part of the congregation. Persons in one goal-task area may show antipathy and hostility toward the goals, tasks, and leaders of another. A congregation is composed of such constituent groups. The wholeness of a congregation is either an effective functioning or nonfunctioning coalition of these constituent groups.

In the contemporary church it is difficult to maintain an effective, functioning coalition. The different goal-task areas are subject to different stresses from the populations they serve and from the environments to which they are exposed. Stewardship committees experience different stress internally and from the community than do youth work committees. Community action committees have different experiences in the congregation and the community from the budget and finance committees. Church organizations respond selectively with resources to different goal-task areas. For example, stewardship and new member committees may be given maximum help and resources while social action and Christian education committees may be thwarted and prevented from making an effective, adequate response to areas of need. In such cases alienation of members of the latter committees is predictable.

INVOLVEMENT OF PERSONS IN THE CHURCH

Since the church is a gathering of strangers, it exhibits a mixture of many kinds and degrees of involvement of persons. How is this variety of involvement to be understood? This book attempts to give an explanation of the panoply of personal involvement.

Our contention is that involvement varies with personal goals, personal goals for the congregation, and congregational goals. Goals are embedded in organizational processes and arrangements. These are the instruments through which a congregation acts to achieve or ignore personal goals. Organizational processes and arrangements are forms of power. The use of power in these forms directly affects the involvement of persons and the support of organizational goals. Most leaders tend to think of power simply as the use of force. Consequently they dismiss the concept as impertinent or useless as a means for thinking about the church. Power is displayed and used in simple, almost invisible ways. Its use lies at the center of our personal and organizational life. The effects of power in a congregation can be seen in the perceptions, feelings, and involvements of persons. The nature and intensity of persons' involvement can be best understood by examining both congregational goals in relation to personal goals, and the use of the various forms of power to achieve congregational goals or the goals of leaders.

If persons have goals which they think are important, these goals assume the force of a moral imperative: "We should," "We ought to." If persons holding goals lack power to attain them, they may calculate and plan ways in which they can achieve them nevertheless. Or they may make statements and engage in actions by which they become increasingly estranged from leaders and other members, behavior that psychologists call "alienative involvement." They may even manifest that ultimate form of alienative involvement, withdrawal. Withdrawal is the most intense and dramatic form of estrangement, but, too frequently the reasons for this act go unnoticed. Leaders respond to pressure groups or caucuses with anxiety and fervor, while they entirely miss the profoundly intense, negative form of alienative involvement, withdrawal, because it is silent.

In developing a description of three types of involvement—moral, calculative, alienative—Etzioni did not suggest that each type is seen in a pure form. There are calculative (planned, cautious, shrewd) and alienative (indifferent, estranged, excluded) behaviors which are profoundly moral. Most behaving in the church is a mixture of calculative, moral, and/or alienative activities. All three types appear in negative and positive forms with varying degrees of intensity.

Moral involvement is the most illusive type in the church. There is much moral rhetoric but little hard thinking about actions and their moral basis. It is assumed that rhetoric produces moral behavior. Not until there is inquiry and reflection about both the quality and the character of the goals of persons and the church, and the ways in which various forms of power are used in relation to these goals, can judgments be made about their morality. The ways in which forms of power are used in relation to goals must be observed. Rhetoric is only one form of individual and organizational behavior. It is not altogether helpful in revealing the morality of either individuals or organizations. But the use of the forms of power is a far more accurate indicator of morality of not only persons but also organizations.

Persons not only behave in calculative, moral, and alienative ways, they also perceive others as behaving in these ways. This understanding in turn affects the nature and intensity of their own future involvement. Involvement in a congregation is influenced by the *perception* of the behaviors of others, and accurate or inaccurate, these perceptions are powerful in shaping the involvement of persons.

A person's perception of how effective a congregation is in attaining goals that are important to him or her increases the positive involvement of that person. A perception of ineffectiveness decreases involvement and may produce intense, negative involvement. Examples of such behavior include developing rival slates for church officers at congregational meetings, resistance to present leadership, apathy, and even withdrawal. The "salted nuts" theory of motivation supports this point. The more a person eats, the more one wants. The more one finds his or her personal goals fulfilled, the more intensely one becomes involved in the life of an organization. A congregation that is effective in achieving its goals affects the involvement of its members positively. The congregation that has no goals, or that sets unrealistic goals for itself and does not attain them, generally experiences lower involvement of members.

Involvement of persons is usually expressed in one of two forms, *expressive* or *instrumental,* in relation to the goals and tasks of a congregation. *Expressively involved persons* generally make speeches, engage in acts of ritual, express feelings and perceptions about ideas, events, plans and projects both in words and actions. These persons tend to attract attention, arouse emotions, and excite others. *Instrumentally involved persons* tend to make motions in meetings, develop plans and strategies, develop alternative solutions and programs, use problem-solving methods of thinking, develop criteria, etc. Goal attainment is frequently frustrated when the wrong type of persons are selected for particular tasks. Passionate speeches may be made, and earnest prayers offered for the attainment of congregational goals, but frustration and apathy result when persons who have the instrumental skills needed to attain the goals are ignored or cannot be found in a congregation.

Since positive involvement increases with effective attainment of goals, leaders should examine both the processes by which persons are selected for task groups and committees, and the educational programs of the church to see if the church is equipping individuals for the variety of congregational tasks. Positive involvement increases as members are personally effective in attaining goals and performing tasks that are important to them.

THE CHURCH—A DIFFUSE POWER SYSTEM

The use of power by the pastor and key leaders has dramatic consequences for the involvement of members. William A. Gamson offers a wide range of observations on the relation between power and discontent, the use of power and the increase of distrust, and the behavior of members when trust decreases.[7] Most church leaders do not identify their activities as acts of power. This is the hidden dimension to leadership. Acts of power are hidden behind words, i.e., influence, "decently and in order," following the rules, doing what is best for the church, doing what we were elected to do. Yet much energy of leaders is spent overcoming the resistance, apathy, discontent of others through focusing on communication of messages to overcome resistance. Problems are diagnosed as problems of communication and content of messages rather than problems of power, leadership style, purpose, values and norms for living as a church, and programs.

Power, when exercised as a hidden dimension in church life, is unexamined. The practices of overcoming the resistance of others in the church are unseen. The alternative understanding and uses of power are unexplored. For example, the use of coercive power (force) increases resistance and each application of such power tends to mobilize and increase counter power. The use of rewards and punishments, utilitarian power, generates less counter power, but assumes that leaders in fact have the rewards and punishments to overcome resistances. The power of values (normative power), particularly when these are commonly shared values, is least alienating of members. Resistance is low among and between those who share the same values. When these commonly shared values are expressed in a common set of expectations for the church and a shared vision (purposes), there is least alienation from and distrust of leaders who use power.[8]

There is yet another unexamined dimension to power in the church. Many leaders tend to assume that power is a static commodity, an entity, which is stable in nature, concentrated in particular locations, and does not change. Persons who assume this understanding of power search for those concentrations of power and seek to attain control of the commodity. The usual pattern is to search for the "power people"—those who have the reputation of having power, influence, the capacity to overcome resistances —and to gain power from the power people. This personal understanding of power ignores a major fact about power; in voluntary organizations power is not only personal but institutional.

Leaders may have much personal power over the most trivial, incidental aspects of a church's life, and be unable to influence the direction or quality of that life, and unable to mobilize significant support even for the basic aspects of church life, including worship.

In contrast to the personal understanding of power, there is an alternative organizational or institutional perspective which maintains that the power of a church to achieve its purposes and to alter the quality of its life is flexible. It contracts and expands. It is dynamic and diffuse. The capacity to overcome resistances and achieve purposes is not concentrated in a small group of persons, but it is ultimately lodged in the whole church whose members must give consent, time, ideas, energy, and money. Members voluntarily give resources. They increase or decrease the resources they share. This accounts for the dynamism and complexity of organizational power. The contracting and expanding character, the flexibility, and the diffuse nature of such power in every member and in each group, severely limits the use of power by leaders who are not seen as legitimate and trusted.

Some leaders have illusions of power, but these illusions disappear as clergy and governing boards attempt to achieve goals that do not have wide support in the congregation. Power is lodged in every member and group. Each person has total control over his piece of power. Control of this power is exercised through attendance and contribution of resources (time, money, ideas, skills) to congregational goals. This is real power, as any budget and finance committee can attest at stewardship time. Personnel committees, after countless calls have produced few church school teachers, committee members, and nominees for church offices, can bear a similar witness. In such a diffuse power system, clergy and leadership groups have only small amounts of total congregational power at their disposal. Few rewards and punishments can be meted out to increase the power of leaders to any substantial amount. Rather, organizational power that is made available to leaders must be developed through activating and mobilizing members. Power to achieve goals within the organization depends upon individuals and constituent groups contributing their power in such a way that leaders can use it. (See Exercise 1.) Persons are much more likely to share power, to contribute their resources, when the congregation incorporates their personal goals into congregational goals and then supports and encourages persons to work to attain these goals. (See Exercise 2.) Persons withhold resources when goal attainment is thwarted, and consequently the power of leaders and the congregation is diminished.

The organizational and personal power available to achieve goals depends on the goals of a congregation, the processes used to determine the goals, and the manner in which forms of power are used by clergy and leadership groups. The involvement of persons and groups in the church increases or decreases as leaders incorporate or disregard personal goals of individuals. Positive and negative attitudes develop toward leaders as members perceive these leaders using delegated forms of power to affect their own personal goals. When apathy and alienation result, ministers and leaders frequently attempt personal methods of motivation (preaching, pastoral calling, inducing guilt feelings, etc.) rather than to alter the forms of power they have been using. Many problems of motivation are not individual in nature but congregational or organizational. We turn in Chapter 4 to an examination of organizational forms of power and the dynamic processes that affect persons and goals.

GOALS AND PRIORITIES
AMONG CONGREGATIONAL LEADERS

1. Develop a list of:
    a. The most important programs in the congregation.
    b. The most important tasks to be done.

2. Develop a ranking (from most important to least important) of:
    a. The programs listed above.
    b. The tasks listed above.

3. By what criteria did you rank these goals and tasks? What aspects of Christian faith were important in the criteria? What significant ideas of Christian faith appear to be missing? How would these ideas alter the criteria and the ranking?

4. Share your ranking of goals and tasks with other leaders. What observations can you make about *(a)* the ranking of goals and tasks; *(b)* the criteria used in ranking; *(c)* the passions and theological commitments represented in the priority goals and tasks of leaders?

5. As leaders, what is your perception about the priority goals and tasks of members of the congregation? Is there congruence in perceptions of members and leaders?

QUESTIONNAIRE ON CONGREGATIONAL GOALS

This instrument is designed to help you indicate your perceptions about the goals of a congregation. There are no right or wrong answers. Check the appropriate space that best expresses your perceptions about the goals.

1. The goals of this congregation are clear to me.
   Agree — $\frac{}{1}$ $\frac{}{2}$ $\frac{}{3}$ $\frac{}{4}$ $\frac{}{5}$ $\frac{}{6}$ $\frac{}{7}$ Disagree

2. The goals of this congregation are not clear.
   Agree — $\frac{}{1}$ $\frac{}{2}$ $\frac{}{3}$ $\frac{}{4}$ $\frac{}{5}$ $\frac{}{6}$ $\frac{}{7}$ Disagree

3. Someone else has established the goals of this congregation.
   Agree — $\frac{}{1}$ $\frac{}{2}$ $\frac{}{3}$ $\frac{}{4}$ $\frac{}{5}$ $\frac{}{6}$ $\frac{}{7}$ Disagree

4. My personal goals are consistent with the goals of this congregation.
   Agree — $\frac{}{1}$ $\frac{}{2}$ $\frac{}{3}$ $\frac{}{4}$ $\frac{}{5}$ $\frac{}{6}$ $\frac{}{7}$ Disagree

5. I have been involved in establishing the goals of this congregation.
   Agree — $\frac{}{1}$ $\frac{}{2}$ $\frac{}{3}$ $\frac{}{4}$ $\frac{}{5}$ $\frac{}{6}$ $\frac{}{7}$ Disagree

6. It is clear to me how we are moving to achieve our goals.
   Agree — $\frac{}{1}$ $\frac{}{2}$ $\frac{}{3}$ $\frac{}{4}$ $\frac{}{5}$ $\frac{}{6}$ $\frac{}{7}$ Disagree

7. The goals of this congregation are unexamined.
   Agree — $\frac{}{1}$ $\frac{}{2}$ $\frac{}{3}$ $\frac{}{4}$ $\frac{}{5}$ $\frac{}{6}$ $\frac{}{7}$ Disagree

In groups of 6 to 8 persons summarize the perceptions on each item. Make a chart so that the group can see all the responses.

What are the most striking features of the group's summary? Which items suggest conditions that could be improved? What else needs to be done?

Develop specific recommendations.

CHAPTER 4

Forms of Power
and Involvement of Persons

Church leaders do not ordinarily ask: What is the impact of the way the church exists and does its work on the perceptions, feelings, and knowledge of members and groups in the church? Nor do leaders ask: "What are the fundamental values undergirding and being expressed in the way the church currently exists and does its work? Where have these values and their forms in concrete life come from historically? Are these values and the expression of these values appropriate to our understanding of Christian faith in this time?

These questions suggest that the church is a profound moral or immoral expression in its very existence, and that the church in its existence and working, completely separate from its rational activities of preaching and teaching, has a significant impact on the being and thinking of people. Members create mental images (perceptions, feelings, and knowledge) of the church and selves as they experience the church in all of its life.

As Western, and now increasingly Eastern, rationalists and individualists, we think that the church is experienced only through words, and that the church's message is conveyed only through words. But concrete actions are messages that persons and groups perceive, know, and feel, and thereby are another meaning in addition to words. The social reality of the church including actions interprets a relation between members and leaders, clergy and laity, members and other members. This relationship is structured through forms of power: structure, politics, or decision-making, polity, control of resources, and communication processes. These forms of power are used to create a concrete reality that establishes relationships and, consequently, the meaning of persons and groups in the church. The forms of power are experienced as qualities of relations, and therefore represent a fundamental value system, or an interpretation of morality.

This chapter is written to assist leaders to examine the forms of power found in church life. These forms are found universally in all churches. The values found in the forms, and the forms of power used in the church are historical creations. They are legacies, for the most part, of the church in different times and cultures when the relations existing between clergy and laity, leaders and members, were substantially different. Earlier church leaders did not have the same values of many members and leaders today. There was a different "fit" between values and forms.

In a gathering of strangers there are many and diverse values and a variety of expectations about the forms of power and the way these forms should be used to reflect members' values. Leaders seek to discern the impact of the church as an existing entity upon members, to understand the values undergirding that which is felt, perceived, and known by members, and to identify the forms of power which have such consequences for members. The response of leaders is to elevate new, more uplifting values, and to work to transform the forms of power to embed new values with new qualities of relations. Each congregation has its own unique structure and organizational characteristics. Structural patterns and accompanying ways of working develop in particular cultures and show the influence of these cultures on the church. There have been no uniquely Christian structures with Christian characteristics. Instead, the church in each historical moment has adopted the organizational style that was dominant in the surrounding culture. Of course, in its more reflective moments the church has made attempts to "Christianize" these cultural contributions. In such cases the church has transformed culture in Christ's name to express Christian truths and perceptions of life. In Figure 2 an attempt has been made to correlate organizational structures in different types of environment with the characteristics associated with these structures. Cultural periods pass and, as each ends, remnants of the culture remain in the structure of church organizations. In fact, organizational structures may pass through several cultural periods which transform various aspects of the organization. In each period new elements may be added and old elements eliminated or modified to fit the new cultural patterns.

Lewis Mumford, in *The Pentagon of Power*, describes the way in which the basic structure of human organizations from the historical period of sun-god worship was adapted to meet the needs of the medieval feudal period.[9] This pyramidal structure in which power was concentrated at the top was subsequently adapted to meet the needs of nineteenth-century industrial, military, and religious organizations. Max Weber has documented this adaptation in his studies of late-nineteenth-century industry, the Roman Catholic Church, and the Prussian Army. The feudal structure served the needs of religious, industrial, and military organizations in a world basically composed of two social classes: the rich who were powerful and the poor who were powerless. But the nineteenth-century adaptation lost its capacity to be the major form of human organization with the emergence of the middle class. Gradually the pyramidal model lost its power in industry when persons at every level had expertise, knowledge, and ability which the owner or managers did not possess. Information and know-how can be translated into power. In rapidly changing environments, organizations needed ideas, new knowledge, and skills in different combinations. Rather than have rigid groupings of specialists working in isolation on a particular piece of equipment or project, new flexible groupings were created which could bring together different experience, knowledge, and skills to provide the necessary resources for solving complex problems. The industrial system, with changing markets and multiple competitors who were inventing new processes and products, could no longer tolerate uninformed, arbitrary, and unilateral decision-making with one-way (i.e., top-down) communication to the worker. Thus a devolution of power has taken place in many industrial organizations. Workers now participate in management planning and decisions.

As organizations have experienced turbulent environments they have altered their structure and other organizational characteristics to gain more resources and better utilize power of workers and members. Characteristics found in many organizations today include increased freedom for members to make responsible decisions on their own, greater cooperation and interdependence between parts of an organization, extensive review and evaluation processes, negotiation or mutual adjustment between persons and groups, increased emphasis on communication in all directions, and visible processes of decision-making. Persons are as fully informed as they need and desire to be.

New matrix and network-tribal models for organizational structure have given contemporary organizations much greater flexibility. They are able to respond both to the needs of the larger society and to the needs of members of the organization who would no longer be satisfied with passive, dependent roles. Managing these contemporary types of organizations is more difficult. It requires different kinds of knowledge and skills than the older types of organizations. Church organizations with the passions of men and women at work, multiple and diverse goals, historical legacies of structure, rules and procedures have difficulty adjusting to rapidly changing environments. Members have an anti-institutional, anti-management bias. And the incessant devolution of power that has been taking place with the termination of feudalism creates an identity crisis in many clergy and laypersons.

As we turn to look more intently at the various forms of power, it is appropriate to see that each form and every organizational characteristic has consequences for persons, as well as for the organization. It needs to be stressed that the church is unavoidably moral, especially in its arrangements and forms of power. The assumption in presenting this material is that church persons can relate to their moralities, and hence to the organizational arrangements they create, and their use of various forms of power.

STRUCTURE

Structures are the arena of "social actions in social space."[10] Leaders and members act to express wills, needs, interests, and values in time and space, but, in addition, the time and space in which they act is an expression of wills, interests, needs, and values. Figure 2 can be used to reflect upon the variety of wills, interests, needs, and values that have informed the creation of structures in different historical moments. Leaders can also use the ideas in this illustration to imagine the impact of different structures with their concomitant characteristics upon the perceptions, feelings, knowledge, and identity of members. Structures create a consciousness in members. They convey a definition of membership or nature of the church. They embody a definition of the purpose of the church. Structures express in powerful ways qualities of life important in the past and in the present. Structuring, therefore, is a most powerful act of expressing values, and the morality of leadership. We turn now to examine structuring more carefully.

FIGURE 2
CHARACTERISTICS ASSOCIATED WITH DIFFERENT ORGANIZATIONAL STRUCTURES

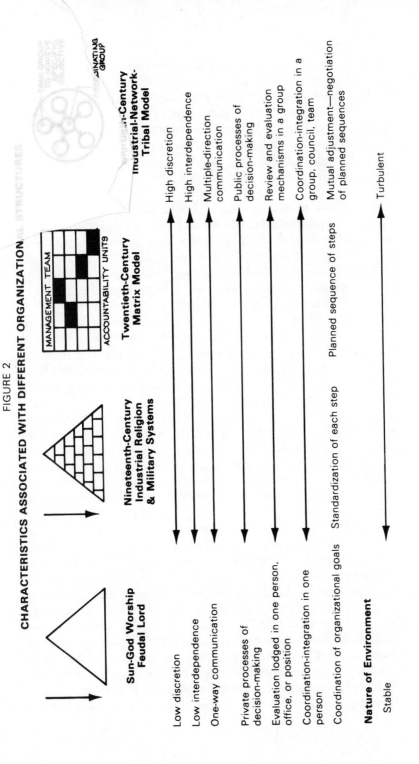

Sun-God Worship Feudal Lord	Nineteenth-Century Industrial Religion & Military Systems	Twentieth-Century Matrix Model	Twenty-first-Century Industrial-Network-Tribal Model
Low discretion	→		High discretion
Low interdependence	→		High interdependence
One-way communication	→		Multiple-direction communication
Private processes of decision-making	→		Public processes of decision-making
Evaluation lodged in one person, office, or position	→		Review and evaluation mechanisms in a group
Coordination-integration in one person	→		Coordination-integration in a group, council, team
Coordination of organizational goals	Standardization of each step	Planned sequence of steps	Mutual adjustment—negotiation of planned sequences

Nature of Environment

Stable	→		Turbulent

Structure is the arrangement of persons and resources in time and space. Persons with passions and goals are ordered in time. Organizations give time, allow persons to have time or no time, and regularize the contribution of persons in a time sequence. Persons and groups are arranged in order of sequence in meetings. These persons and groups are adjusted with space between them through agendas, schedules, planning processes, and location of meetings. The result is that not all persons can contribute resources.

Resources—including persons, money, ideas, and organizational support and encouragement—are allotted and distributed to certain individuals and groups. Persons and groups have different degrees of access to resources. Some persons are located with ready access to what they need for their tasks. Others are deprived not only of the resources, but even of knowledge that resources exist in different parts of a congregation.

The creation of a structure for a congregation is a vital and necessary function. No congregation can exist without structure, but creating a structure is always a powerful act. The structure expresses the values and commitments of the powerful, and it has consequences for both the more powerful and the less powerful. The creators of structure are generally placed in a posture of justifying their particular arrangement of persons and resources in time and space. The less powerful, if they sense an injustice or an inadequacy in the structure, challenge the values and judgments of the creators. The more intensely personal goals and personal goals for the congregation are held, and the more they differ from those goals of the creators of the structure, the greater will be their challenge to the judgments of those who order and arrange.

Structure is the most visible expression of how a ruling group deals with the goals of persons and of the congregation. Both the motivation and the involvement of persons are affected by structure. When a structure does not help members achieve goals that are important to them and their groups, then intense involvements of various types are possible. (See Figure 1.) Both apathy and active political effort to replace those in power are intense forms of involvement responsive to structural isolation of persons, resources, and goals. Active, positive involvement follows from structural arrangements that encourage persons to work effectively on personal and organizational goals important to them. Persons perceive they have power and therefore tend to be involved positively when the structure makes needed resources available to attain their goals. Powerlessness and its consequent alienative involvement are most evident when persons are structured at a distance in time and space from decision-making and from the allotment of resources. Persons feel, perceive, and know the effects of the structure of a congregation on them and their goals.

The diffused assignment of persons and resources to different parts of the program means that power is diffused. If goals are important to persons in a particular part, these persons compete with persons from other parts for the limited resources available. A power struggle that affects the involvement of persons ensues. Conflict between the worship committee and the Christian education committee is commonplace, particularly when the congregation has a "paid" choir. The Christian education committee argues that the money spent for soloists and choir members could be better spent on teaching resources. If the minister and/or decision-making group decide in favor of the Christian education committee and its program, the choir may transfer to another congregation, seek to have the minister fired, or politicize the congregation and work to elect a new group of church officers who will render a more favorable decision. If the leadership group decides in favor of the choir, the Christian education committee may show the same alienative involvement.

This dynamic behavior of parts of a congregation points to the reality of diffused power. No group of leaders or decision makers has all the power needed to effect its will arbitrarily or unilaterally. Few congregations accept the leadership of a single group of elected "representatives" to make decisions that affect the goals of a congregation. Therefore there is competition and often conflict between persons in different parts of a congregation's program. Each area has its goals, tasks, and functions. Persons join one or another because they agree with the goals and think the tasks important, and after becoming involved they often become increasingly motivated to attain those goals. There are instances where persons are misplaced or become alienated, so that apathy or hostility to leaders is manifest. Conflict between leaders of different parts of a congregation that have different goals and unequal amounts of resources is an important phenomenon of congregational behavior.

UNDERSTANDING THE STRUCTURE OF A CONGREGATION

The study of the structure of a congregation reveals what actually exists and therefore that which a leadership group must manage wisely and well. There is a tendency to blame persons in the different parts of a congregation when tension and conflict are found. Rarely do persons look at the structure of a congregation for clues as to why disturbances arise. Exercise 3 is provided to assist leaders to get hold of the structure. In this exercise it will be seen that each part has tasks to perform in relation to the congregational goals. Leaders will want answers to the following questions: Is there clarity in the leadership groups and among members in each part as to what the principal tasks are? If there is lack of clarity by either party, what typical responses might be expected?

Each area of congregational activity and program has drawn particular types of persons and groups into that area. For example, the Sunday morning Bible-study class may be composed mainly of persons over fifty-five years of age, male and female, with an average annual income over $15,000, graduates of high school who are well known and respected in the community. Such persons also form the majority of members of the governing board of the congregation. In contrast, the Committee for Establishing a Day Care Center may be composed of females under forty-five years of age with husbands who have an income of approximately $20,000 annually, and both husbands and wives are college or university graduates. These persons are new residents to the community (average six years in the community), and they are known primarily by a small group of like-minded persons in the congregation who are concerned primarily with the church's mission in the community.

The environment in which each of the above groups seeks to accomplish its tasks differs remarkably. Dr. Barnes's Bible Class may have been created when the present members were young. The class has been a stable life experience for them. The task environment of Dr. Barnes's class is quite stable and homogeneous. The most disruptive element in the class is the death of its members as they grow older. The Committee for Establishing a Day Care Center experiences an entirely different world in seeking to accomplish its task. The leadership group in the church is ambiguous and uncommitted to their goal. City and state laws

specifying building and teacher requirements, the prospect of no
funding or minimal funding from the congregation, Federal Government funding policies, community social agency requirements, and the desires of parents of children in the proposed day
care center constitute a rapidly shifting and heterogeneous environment. Each part of a congregation experiences a radically different environment in which to function.

The major tools required by each group to accomplish its task
also differ significantly. Dr. Barnes's Bible Class needs Bibles, perhaps a commentary or two, and a blackboard. Members of the class
know what is needed. Members of the Day Care Center Committee need knowledge of city, state, and federal laws, policies of
community agencies, fund-raising, budgeting, planning, organizing, management, and public relations skills. They need knowledge of their prospective constituents, and perhaps knowledge of
the political influence patterns in the church and community. The
committee may or may not have the knowledge and tools needed.
It may not know what it needs to know and what tools it needs for
its task. Environmental elements may continue to shift as laws are
changed and the budget priorities of community agencies are
altered each year. The knowledge and tools (technology) needed
by each part differ and may change dramatically for some parts as
the environment changes.

Dr. Barnes and his class meet every Sunday morning in a room
that has their name on the door. No one will question their meeting. They have a high degree of discretion. They may continue for
years without any additional approval or evaluation. The governing board is grateful for their offering and loyalty to the church.
The minister may be concerned about the way in which the Bible
is studied, and there may be official concern expressed about the
class, if it appears that the class is becoming a substitute for attendance at Sunday morning worship. But it is perceived as doing what
a church group ought to be doing and, therefore, has authority and
sanction to do it. On the other hand, the Day Care Center Committee may have been created because a young wife of a member
of the governing board wrote a passionate letter to the board
describing the need and conditions in the community that call for
this ministry of the church. The husband and minister supported
the plea, and the formation of a committee was approved and
subsequently appointed. But what was it appointed to do? Study?
Plan? Implement? The committee may think that it was appointed to create a day care center. The governing board, on the

EXERCISE 3

UNDERSTANDING THE STRUCTURE
OF THE CONGREGATION

1. On a blackboard or large sheet of newsprint make a five-column chart similar to the following:

I	II	III	IV	V
Organization or Committee	Major Goal	Characteristics of Participants	Needed Tools and Resources	Authority Given and Resources Provided

2. With the assistance of all present fill in the chart in the following manner:

   a. In Column I list all the organizations and committees in the congregation.
   b. In Column II state the principal task or goal of each.
   c. In Column III summarize the dominant characteristics of participants as to age, sex, income, status in church and community, homogeneity, and continuity.
   d. In Column IV list the tools and resources needed to accomplish the goal.
   e. In Column V list the authority given and resources available to each organization and committee.

3. When the chart has been completed, discuss such questions as the following:

   a. In what respects does the organized life of the congregation reflect the makeup of the congregation?
   b. How faithfully do the goals of the organizations and committees embody the goals of the congregation, the members' goals for the congregation, and the members' personal goals?
   c. In what ways does this structure limit the full participation of members?
   d. Are tools and resources distributed adequately?
   e. What areas of congregational life require more attention by policy makers and leaders?

other hand, may have appointed the committee to study, with the implicit belief that nothing would ever come of it. The authority of the committee is low. It has almost no discretion to act. Officially, it is authorized and expected to do nothing.

Tension and frustration in the Day Care Committee are predictable. They are prepared to find "enemies" inside and outside the church. The behavior of Dr. Barnes's Class is equally predictable. Different parts of a congregation have different tasks, persons, and environments. They need different knowledge and tools to accomplish their tasks. The amount of discretion allowed each part varies with the goals of the church, the goals of the governing board, the characteristics of persons in the part (Who are they? Are they trustworthy?) and the resources needed and available. The management of this diversity by a governing board is a major challenge to the health and effectiveness of the congregation in ministry and mission.

Structure affects the behavior of persons, groups, and the congregation. Therefore the nature of structures in congregations requires positive, attentive governance. Structure cannot be taken for granted. It affects the involvement of all members and church professionals. As the governing board makes decisions about structure, it affects every aspect of the congregation's life and the involvement of persons in it. Many governing boards are hesitant to examine their style of governing and the effects of structure on the behavior of persons, groups, the congregation, and the achievement of congregational goals.

POLITICAL ACTIVITY AND CONGREGATIONAL BEHAVIOR

Political activity as such is not new to the church. However, in recent years it has been increasingly visible. As its visibility has increased, controversy has developed. New groups are becoming politically active and Keith Bridston, a Lutheran layman, in his book *Church Politics*,[11] encourages such activity. There is disdain from others because it is not considered "spiritual" to engage in political activity. In many instances, these persons have engaged in the politics of elite minority rule, but are now challenged by various persons and groups in a congregation.

Bridston calls for the creation of political parties within the church to do the church's business. A denomination, such as his, has an ethnic background, a history of limited participation by laity and clergy in church decision-making, and a fairly stable environment in the more northern rural areas of the country. Decisions are often made by a few senior, elite, and powerful clergy with a few elite laymen concurring. Bridston forcefully challenges elite minority rule. Clergy and laity from other denominations read his book and identify with the conditions which he describes and the prescription he has made. The political caucus has become a favored style to organize and challenge the old political rule. But the challenged elite look at the political caucus and decry political activity, without a trace of recognition of the political activity in which they have engaged. By means of informal caucuses, luncheon meetings, telephone calls, they have controlled nominating committee meetings, and appointments to key positions and offices.

Attention to church politics is not confined to the discontented. The late Alan Richardson, Dean of York, an elite minority decision maker in the Church of England, noted the rise of interest in political activity in the church. He responded by writing *The Political Christ*,[12] a study of the political involvement of Jesus and the early church. Reflecting attitudes and movements in the larger society, men and women in the church have engaged increasingly in this activity to attain their personal goals and personal goals for the church. Political involvement is one of the forms of power. The discontented engage in political activity as a response to this activity by others. When one looks at a congregation or other type of church organization and sees political caucuses, there is need to look at the style of political activity which has been practiced in the past to understand the present response to that activity. Political activity calls forth this type of involvement as a response. Frequently the behavior that leaders dislike or are fearful of has appeared as a reaction to the political style and activity of the present leadership. Leaders are generally unaware that their own behavior tends to produce the behavior they dislike in others. It is much easier to find "enemies" than to examine what a particular style of political activity has produced in the membership. Political styles of involvement invariably produce political enemies. Political activity is a form of organizational behavior that has consequences for the involvement, attitudes, and feelings of both clergy and laypersons.

There are two predominant styles of political activity in the church today: the structuralist and the pluralist.[13] Each style has its unique impact on the behavior of a congregation. The structuralist style is certainly better known and more easily recognizable in the church. Every denomination has its roots in this style of political activity, since denominations began in countries with kings and queens, godly and ungodly princes, Protestant and Catholic lords, earls and patrons. These persons, by virtue of their ownership of the land, owned the church as well and operated it as a magnificent patronage system that returned income on investment. The political system was seldom challenged except when the godly prince became ungodly. That meant he was Catholic in the midst of Protestant lords, or Protestant in the middle of Catholic lords. As long as the ruling elite, kings and queens, or pope reflected and supported even in minimal ways the prevailing values, attitudes, and ideas of the powerful lords, the political system was not challenged. It mattered little how the serfs, tenants, and ordinary people in the church felt. The godly prince and his supporting powerful lords could make unchallenged decisions.

Bridston and others who challenge the present political system in the church claim they are challenging the godly princes of today. These they describe as those power figures who form an elite minority rule in congregations, synods, presbyteries, districts, and dioceses. These "princes" feel an enormous pressure and antagonism from multiple directions to bring their reign to an end. The behavior of the organization tends to produce responsive behaviors in the ruling elite.

We need to look carefully at these styles of political activity and their characteristics. (See Figure 3.) What kind of behavior does each tend to call forth in professional church workers, governing boards and groups? How do they influence relations between groups, and effect the ministry and mission goals of the church?

Members who practice the two political styles recognize in common the existence of unequal priorities and power, the inertia and apathy of large numbers of members, and the inadequacy of the rules and procedures (polity) of most congregations to maintain an adequate check on the behavior of groups and members. Groups and individuals tend to ignore books of discipline and order, except to use them to thwart the aims of other persons and groups.

There are few, if any, congregations or other types of church organizations where either a structuralist or a pluralist style of political activity can be found in a "textbook" form.

It is important to understand not only the two dominant types of political activity but also the effects of these styles. Figure 4 contains a comparison of the possible effects of the two different styles of political activity on the pastor, the governing board, the

FIGURE 3

CHARACTERISTICS OF TWO POLITICAL STYLES COMPARED

Structuralist Emphases	**Pluralist Emphases**
Decision-making by small group in control	Decision-making by multiple groups in process.
Assumes static, closed system to face challenges.	Assumes dynamic, open, challengeable systems.
Rule by elite minority.	Rule by coalition of minorities.
Continual assertion of interests by minority group of leaders.	Problem of various individuals and groups agreeing on interests.
Power lodged in minority group.	Power diffused in various coalition groups.
Maintains perspective over total congregation in order to assert interests.	Tendency to lose total perspective in asserting special interests.
Change through slow adaptation, which should not be forced if best results are to be obtained.	Change through organizing minority groups for concerted effort in situations that cannot be ignored.
Assumes a silent, invisible, or covert elite leadership group.	Assumes an elite group, resulting from a coalition of groups holding power on one or more issues.
Power centers in elite leadership group enabling them continually to assert their interests.	No group without some form of social power, nor individual without resources that can be mobilized.

congregation, and ministry and mission goals. It is a summary of responses of clergy and laity in congregations that have experienced either of the two styles.

There are implications for a congregation in the use of a particular political style. In comparing the two styles, one can readily see the effects of each on involvement of persons and their resources. Most congregations have enormous potential power and resources that are never actualized. A political style effects the way potential resources are put to use in the church. Political activity as a form of power is related directly to negative or positive involvement of members and the intensity of that involvement in a congregation.

With the increasing diversity of personal goals and personal goals for the congregation, it is imperative that there be a political style that encourages the development of openness and visibility of these differences and enables minority groups to form coalitions and be active politically without being labeled "enemies." Coalitions do not necessarily imply intense, abrasive activity. They can mean new cooperation and interdependency if there can be public forums where persons can get information about the variety of goals possible for a congregation, and where they can develop a common understanding about these goals. This does not mean that universal agreement must be sought for every goal and objective, but there must be understanding about what they mean and what they signify for others. In many congregations today, persons do not find the opportunity to support their own goals in positive political action, or to understand and support the goals of others.

A minority group representing a narrow range of interests will not be able to rule wisely and well in a turbulent, diverse congregation. The only majority that exists in most congregations is composed of the apathetic and inactive members. A governing board must represent the diverse interests of the entire congregation and there must be public occasions when all members can seek to understand and support, as much as possible, the goals of others.

In congregations where groups of persons supporting goals are each a minority, the structuralist style of control and the more radical or revolutionary political style of overthrow are inappropriate. Competing groups and organizations call for a pluralistic style of rule if justice and love are to be served. To seek a political style that activates God's people, opens them up to the diversity of minority groups and the unique resources of individuals, and engages them in reflection about common purposes, even when they do not have much in common, is a legitimate goal of leaders.

FIGURE 4

**POSSIBLE CONSEQUENCES OF
STRUCTURALIST AND PLURALIST STYLES**

FOR THE PASTOR

Structuralist	**Pluralist**
Goals, priorities, and behavior influenced by elite minority.	Freedom to pursue various goals represented by individuals and groups.
Lack of response when goals of elite and pastor differ.	Stimulation of competition over goals by persons and groups with different interests.
Frustration over failure to achieve goals for congregation when different from elite's goals.	Frustration over inability to manage coalition of conflicting interests and goals.
Diminishing concern for the interests of the total congregation.	Sense of loss of control over the total congregation.
Alienation from the congregation.	Alienation from minority groups who do not get what they seek.
Tendency to manipulate governing group.	More time spent in planning, managing conflict, and assisting groups to attain their goals.
Tendency to sell out and go along with those in control.	Challenge to experiment with those who want to try new things.
Tendency to move on and let someone else try.	Greater sense of accomplishment with programs that work.

continued

FIGURE 4 (continued)

FOR THE GOVERNING BOARD

Structuralist	Pluralist
No felt need to respond to disparate groups in the congregation.	Possible felt need to listen too much and feel the risks of leadership.
Exaggerated sense of power: "We were elected to run the church."	Increased responsiveness to interests and needs of the congregation.
Commitment to preserving traditional structures and processes.	More openness to change and willingness to experiment.
Possible defensive response to criticism and challenge of what is.	Increased discussion of goals, problems, and issues of the congregation.
Tendency to control nomination and election processes.	Nomination and election processes more responsive to congregational interests.
Tendency to manage information-sharing procedures.	Encouragement of open communication in the congregation.

continued

FIGURE 4 *(continued)*

FOR THE CONGREGATION

Structuralist	Pluralist
Minister is viewed as the generator of new ideas.	New ideas arise out of the diverse interests of the congregation.
Groups with particular concerns will appeal to board through the pastor.	Groups with special concerns will raise them directly with the board.
Interest and involvement falls when a particular interest fails to win support.	Individuals and groups may continue to press their claims for consideration and support.
Programs unpopular with present leadership stand little chance of receiving consideration for resourcing.	Priorities and resourcing are worked out in open competition between individuals and groups.
Members are likely to find personal fulfillment by becoming involved in activities outside the congregation.	Members are likely to become more involved in congregational programs that they have a voice in shaping.
Election of officers likely to be perfunctory with low-level participation, or tense with alternative slates.	Elections likely to be spirited, with high participation and open competition.
Stewardship support likely to come from a relatively small but loyal percent of the members.	Stewardship support will likely be more widely representative of the congregation.
The work of the church will be done by the loyal, overworked few.	Workers for a more diverse program will be found among those interested in particular parts of the program.
Tendency for caucuses and organizations to develop around neglected interests.	Increased participation in setting goals and priorities lessens the need for splinter groups.
Tendency to maintain traditional goals and programs after they have lost their effectiveness.	New ministry and mission goals reflect current interests and needs of the congregation.
Tendency to avoid critical examination of existing goals and programs.	Increased opportunity to criticize all mission goals and programs.

RULES AND PROCEDURES: DO THEY HELP OR HINDER?

There is a strange naivete in the church about polity, the rules and procedures for doing its business. On the one hand, there is little questioning as to whether rules and procedures really enable the congregation to achieve its goals. On the other hand, there is an almost blind acceptance of them and a great commitment to defend them against all who propose even minor alterations. The defenders declare that the business of the church must be done "decently and in order," and assume that the existing rules and procedures present the only possibility for doing so.

Presbyterians call their rules and procedures Presbyterian with
the implication that they would no longer be Presbyterians if their rules and procedures were altered. Baptists and Covenanters make the same claim. When one sits in the solemn assemblies of sessions, councils, administrative and other governing boards, of whatever denomination, they all manifest an amazing similarity. They all lead to dull, boring, ritualistic meetings that are filled with the pretension of actually doing something. Generally they accomplish so little as to be meaningless and a waste of time.

There are differences in polity that affect Baptism, Communion, the interpretation of Scripture, etc. However, it is not these rules and procedures which render the church ineffective. It is rather the rules and procedures that affect the participation of persons in the church and church meetings.

Most rules and procedures were not designed to mobilize or activate members of a congregation. They were designed to maintain control by an elite minority. Present members of governing boards did not design the rules, nor are they particularly satisfied with apathy or discontent which are the signs of ineffective participation. In governing boards where there is more effective participation, church polity is often ignored. Constitutions and bylaws are treated with "benign neglect." Both clergy and laity discover the real dilemma; they desire to be "good" Presbyterians, Methodists, or Baptists and live by the rules; yet they know within themselves that traditional procedures and rules do not mobilize or activate persons for ministry and mission.

The function of polity in each generation has been to facilitate the work of the church. Such procedures and rules are human inventions that enable the church to achieve its goals in a particular era. The rules and procedures found in constitutions, bylaws, and books of order are simply the codification of the methods by which an organization operates. We come to expect that this is the way people ought to act and will act in a congregation. After such methods and expectations have developed, it is possible to write them as standards for an organization and to maintain the expectation that persons will be guided and governed by them. But rules and procedures do not come from God on the wings of an angel. They are creations of persons in a particular historical moment who are attempting to live faithful and obedient lives.

Ministers and laity find it impossible to accomplish much in the church when persons simply do not accept old rules and procedures for participation, when the old standards no longer reflect the behavior and expectations of people. Rules function only as long as ministers and laity will let them function. This means that persons must genuinely feel that particular rules and procedures effectively enable them to attain their personal goals and personal goals for the church.

Anarchy is one major result of attempting to govern a church or a society in which there are no rules or procedures for effective participation. It also appears where the members of a congregation no longer support traditional rules and procedures. When this occurs standard procedures are discarded. Every person does his or her own thing without regard to neighbor or God. For polity to be effective it must provide a means for participation and achievement of goals. Since many persons simply do not believe that present rules and procedures in the church are effective for them, they alter their pattern of involvement to forms of alienative involvement.

Discontent with polity is not local and momentary. The desire for more effective and different kinds of participation is a world-wide phenomenon which is growing in the church. It is not satisfactory to treat it with neglect while muddling through from one crisis after another. Anarchy is not a satisfactory solution. Doing one's own thing runs counter to the most central features of Christian faith, which stress relations to neighbors as a sign of one's relation to God. Polity consists of ways of relating to neighbors and, therefore, to God. It cannot be ignored. For this reason it is most important that we examine and understand the rules and procedures of congregation and attempt to discern alternative processes for developing effective member participation and achievement of goals.

There is genuine tension today between those who hold two

different concepts of polity. For the sake of clarity and comparison, these two views of polity are presented in Figure 5. It should be noted in examining these two perspectives that neither exists in pure form. There is an evolutionary development in most congregations and church organizations. There is tension between those who would change a particular aspect of polity and those who hold that a traditional denominational rule, procedure, or position is the significant element in a denomination and therefore resist strongly any attempts to alter it.

These distinctions are presented descriptively, not disparagingly. There are persons of intelligence and goodwill on both sides because they hold fundamentally different theological assumptions.

Those who are committed to a form of traditional polity tend to believe that God is at work primarily in the church, or the primary focus is God's work in the church. This church, as a human organization, is not substantially affected by the environment, or if it is, the effects can be safely ignored. The church has sufficient internal resources to meet its needs and do its work. Since the primary focus is on the church and its work, undesired influences from the environment should be resisted by sealing off the church membership from these influences. Through such sealing off, the purity of the church can be maintained and the church will be more effective in both its ministry and its mission.

On the other hand, those who hold that new forms of polity are needed believe that God is at work both in the church and in the world. God is at work in the environment that surrounds the church. The environment, where God is also at work, influences the church. Resources that are needed to achieve the congregation's goals are in the environment. There are both positive and negative influences there. Negative influences should be resisted, but such resistance requires discernment from within the church as to what God is doing both within the church and in the world.

Most contemporary polities assume that within the church, persons discern God at work in the church and in the world in different ways; therefore, public processes of goal-setting, planning, and evaluation are needed. Discernment is an activity of God's people, not just of the minister and/or governing board.

Ministers and laity are caught between these two views of polity. In some congregations, the minister and one group of members are committed to one way of doing the church's business, while another group is equally committed to alternative

FIGURE 5

CHARACTERISTICS OF TWO TYPES OF POLITY

Traditional Emphases	New Emphases
Historical creeds provide the authoritative standard of church membership.	New creeds are written in an effort to apply the historic faith to contemporary issues.
Subscription to a particular confession required for officers and members.	Various creeds and confessions regarded as helpful to theological and ethical inquiry by all members.
Traditional rules and procedures regarded as useful in all times and places.	Members are encouraged to think and act as Christians and use the most appropriate tools and methods for doing so.
Broad authority is vested in the minister and governing board.	Goals and procedures are determined with congregation being involved.
Historical precedent often cited to legitimize existing rules and procedures.	Goals, rules, and procedures legitimized through public goal-setting, planning, and evaluation.
Participative behavior guided by constitutions, bylaws, and manuals.	Consensus-forming procedures develop norms for congregational behavior.
Major initiatives rest upon the minister and governing board.	Individuals and groups in congregation are free to initiate goals and programs.
Assumes a passive interest in members of the congregation.	Assumes an active interest in members of the congregation.
Assumes a stable environment for the church.	Assumes a changing, even turbulent environment for the church.
Assumes that existing structures and procedures are adequate.	Assumes that flexible structures and procedures are necessary.
Assumes that goals are clear, known, and attainable.	Assumes that goals are complex, ambiguous, and the means for achieving them uncertain.
Assumes that officers who understand their responsibilities are equipped to fulfill them.	Assumes that leaders, officers, and members need continuing development of understanding and skill for working together, utilizing resources, and achieving goals.

polity. Polity is at the heart of power and involvement of persons in congregational life. The old polity, no matter how comfortable it may feel and how right some of its assumptions appear to be, will not mobilize persons or encourage all members of a congregation to engage in the active discernment of God's will for the church and the world.

The alternatives to traditional polity, historical precedent, and written rules are many: increased human communication; new resources for theological reflection about challenges to faith and life; various ways to hear from constituent groups; planning; processes for arriving at consensus; political processes that mobilize persons and bring other persons and groups into decision-making; leadership development; organizational development; various human relations skills; and evaluation of the quality of congregational life and achievement. When traditional rules and historical resources no longer suffice, a new understanding of polity must emerge that enables persons through communication and decision-making processes to deal effectively with those issues and goals that are most divisive. The old polity cannot hold the diverse groups and their goals together. New polity that enables persons to deal with issues and goals must be substituted. Written rules must be supplemented and, perhaps, supplanted by processes that encourage inquiry, debate, and discussion. In this way a new consensus arises out of the commitment of persons to goals and issues rather than to an organization and its historical way of maintaining an order that developed in a more stable, simple society.

Polity affects the participation of persons and groups and the effectiveness of the congregation in achieving its goals. It is a form of power that needs to be examined and transformed to enable the congregation to be more faithful to its Christian perceptions about life. Christian faith should find expressions in the most concrete forms of congregational life. The rules and procedures by which it does its work are such concrete forms. (See Exercise 4.)

CONTROL OF RESOURCES

Control of resources directly affects the type and intensity of a person's involvement in an organization (e.g., the church). If personal goals are important, then readily available resources to achieve these goals tend to result in members who are intensively and positively involved. This type of involvement is also seen when limited congregational resources are distributed equitably,

EXERCISE 4
A FRESH LOOK AT CONGREGATIONAL
RULES AND PROCEDURES

1. Read the characteristics of the old and new polities in Figure 5. Develop a profile of the rules and procedures of your congregation through reading the bylaws, constitution, manual of procedure, and other helpful documents. Also reflect on your personal experience while participating in meetings and upon the attitudes of the congregation.

2. Are the rules and procedures described in the official documents being followed?

3. Do the rules and procedures encourage and make effective participation possible by ministers, leaders, and all members? You may desire to talk with different groups of members to obtain their perspective on the effects on them of current rules and procedures.

4. What are the strengths of present polity? What alterations could be made to encourage persons and groups to become more effective members?

when there are processes for determining the priority of common congregational goals and for distributing the limited resources available to achieve them.

When distribution of resources is perceived as inequitable or arbitrary, or when the processes for making decisions about distribution are unclear, or when it is felt that the processes for making decisions make use of questionable criteria, then negative, alienative involvement increases. With the diminution of resources in congregations and other types of church organizations, persons who have a high degree of commitment to their goals are sensitive both to the actual distribution of resources and the processes by which such decisions are made.

Resources of a congregation are far more extensive than most persons see. They include time of professionals and laity, energy of members, ideas, skills, tools, information, money, and property. The latter resources, money and property, are the most visible; consequently, greater attention is given to them. But the human, personal resources are the greatest in amount, and their use or misuse is frequently the source of tension and frustration.

If a resources distribution inventory is made, it will be seen that human and physical resources are distributed unevenly. The pattern of distribution may have no correlation, or an inverse one, with the *stated* priority goals of a congregation. Traditional patterns of distribution may prevail, even though the congregation and governing board have established new priorities. Church budgets are not generally informative about how resources are distributed in relation to priority goals. Rather, they are presented in a public-relations advertising fashion as a psychological tool to raise money. Budget makers attempt to hide costs of items in the budget, i.e., salaries of different professional staff, program costs, building maintenance costs. But when information is absent, persons tend to suspect inequities even though none may exist. Therefore *perceptions* about distribution affect involvement, as well as information about the actual distribution. It is more appropriate in the Christian church to tell the truth and let congregations and governing boards together agonize, reflect, and make the hard decisions about how resources are to be allocated. If the congregation is involved in making decisions, it is more likely that additional resources will become available. *Pro forma* budgets, budgets that are adopted from year to year with only minor changes, tell little about actual resource distribution in relation to common congregational priority goals.

In order to activate the church, the distribution of both human and physical resources should be studied in relation to the purposes of the congregation, for patterns of distribution affect the behavior of the congregation, committees, groups, and individuals and have direct consequences for programs and projects.

Careful examination of the distribution of human resources is also important to wise rule in the church. The time of church professionals and laity has become increasingly important. Time may be a more accurate indication of priority and commitment than physical resources. As the goals of a congregation correlate less with personal goals, persons give less time to the congregation. This is true of both ministers and laity. Many clergy have "found" their ministry to be increasingly in the community, working with service clubs, denominational committees, or even writing books. Laypersons devote increasing amounts of time to local community action groups, independent evangelistic groups, and caucus groups in the local congregation, which seem to be external to the congregation's major stated purposes and directions.

Most laypersons do not have accurate information about how the minister actually spends his or her time. Ministers themselves are not always aware, except vaguely, of how their use of time correlates with the priority goals and purposes of the congregation. When information is lacking, persons supply their own interpretation of what is going on, if they care about the congregation and their own personal goals. The interpretation may or may not be accurate.

Much of the current frustration among ministers and laity is due to the amount of time spent on aspects of ministry that seem to bear little relationship to personal priorities, or even to congregational priority goals. Most committees and governing boards have not done a study of the use of time and how this use correlates with personal and congregational priorities. Time is used indiscriminately. Agendas of meetings often do not reflect priority goals, but rather are merely a traditional ordering of items or, even worse, an indiscriminate collection of items which may or may not belong on the agenda.

Church professionals and lay members perceive that their time is worth more when it is used to achieve priority goals of the congregation, particularly when the congregational goals reflect their personal goals for the congregation.

Many priority congregational goals are not achieved because church professionals, governing boards, and committees have not given them priority in the use of their time. Traditional items and programs continue to receive the same attention in spite of contrary decisions that have been made by governing boards, committees, and congregations. How time is actually used indicates the true priorities of church professionals, governing boards, and committees.

Both laity and church professionals chafe because the congregation expects priority goals to be implemented, but still expects ministers, governing boards, and committees to do everything that has been done in the past. Professionals are expected to continue all familiar activities, *and* implement new programs and projects that are important to the congregations. Governing boards are expected both to maintain the traditional activities *and* to implement vital, new programs which require large amounts of human resources.

Few expect professionals and governing boards to make decisions that redistribute human or physical resources. Ministers and governing boards are not clear that incisive decisions must be made to redistribute resources when a new goal becomes a priority. Few are able to decide actually to terminate a program because it is no longer a priority goal of ministry and mission in the congregation. The inability to make such a decision is frequently due to a lack of specific information about how time and other resources are currently distributed and what the achievement of new goals requires. If this information is not known to the congregations, decisions frequently appear to be arbitrary and capricious.

Time and the distribution of time are measurable. Groups and personal energy levels, the number, quality, and flow of ideas, and the use of a congregation's skills for achieving congregational goals also indicate the available human resources of a congregation. However, they are much more difficult to measure. Varying amounts of energy as well as time are given to different goals, programs, and activities. When ideas for achieving goals are not sought, they remain hidden in individuals who could contribute if they were encouraged to participate. But few congregations have processes for encouraging the congregation to contribute ideas. Announcements from the pulpit or in the church bulletin are insufficient to mobilize most persons and their ideas. Skills and tools for implementing programs are virtually unknown. Churches depend upon persons volunteering such information, but most persons are reticent and fail to volunteer. Congregational leaders are also unclear as to which skills and tools are needed, so that it is impossible to approach particular persons for the contribution of their resources.

When persons perceive a low energy level in a program, activity, or goal area that is important to them, negative assessments begin and the basis for alienative involvement is laid. Or when ministers and leaders are seen as closed to ideas from the congregation, persons begin to withdraw their resources of time, money, and skills from the congregation. Leadership is judged inept when the skills and tools necessary for the effective attainment of goals are misused, unused, or alienated.

The perceived inability of leadership groups to distribute or redistribute resources to achieve congregational goals effectively is a major source of discontent in the church. More awareness and conscious intent is needed in the control and allocation of resources. Much more attention must be given to channel human and physical resources where they can best achieve congregational priority goals. This is particularly true when resources decline because of inflation, apathy of members, etc.

Most leadership groups today are faced with a decline in physical resources: money. The precursor to such a decline—a real
decline in human resources: time, ideas, energy, skills and tools of
persons—is not so obvious to leaders. Therefore, leadership groups
respond primarily to the decline in physical resources and not to
the decline in human resources. Processes are needed for mobilizing congregations which elicit personal goals and personal goals
for the church, and which organize persons to work in the areas
most important to them.

In periods of decline of resources no leadership group can appear to be doing its work well unless its mandate from the congregation is clear. No other basis for redistribution of resources will
work. Without a clear decision by the congregation for resource
allocation the special interests of one group or another within the
congregation will feel slighted. No leadership group can escape
redistributing the resources of a congregation in times of declining
support. Congregations with diverse groups of members require
examination again and again of what church professionals, leaders,
and committees do with their time, energy, ideas, skills, tools, and
money from the congregation.

INFORMATION AS A RESOURCE

Perhaps the activity of clergy and lay leaders that most dramatically affects the behavior of individuals, groups, and the church is
control of information. Leadership influences not only the content
of information but also the ways information is received and
shared. In this section the primary focus is upon the effect of
patterns and processes of information-receiving and information-
sharing. (For a visual representation of different patterns of information-sharing, see Exercise 5.)

Leaders need also to examine the nature of information which
they value receiving and sharing. Most leaders prefer information
that affirms their own presuppositions about the way the church
ought to run and is running, rather than information that checks
their assumptions and that brings new information about real conditions in church and community life. Consequently, information-
receiving and information-sharing processes and patterns are
maintained which limit the kinds of information available to leaders, and which control access of members with challenging information to leaders. It takes extraordinary effort by members with

new and different information to communicate with leaders when these leaders control both the content of information that can reach them and the means of access with that information.

Content or the patterns of sharing information have an impact regardless of the character or personality of persons who do the sharing. The way information is shared influences the energy, feelings, and perceptions of persons and groups. This is true even if all the persons sharing information are "good" Christians. Information as a resource is affected primarily by persons' perceptions as to how their own information is handled. It is not the actual pattern of sharing which is important, or the leader's concept of how the information was shared. The perceptions of members, accurate or inaccurate, influence their involvement in the congregation. And how information is shared influences their perceptions.

Perhaps the most appropriate way to understand the simplicity and power of patterns of sharing is to do Exercise 5. (Church officer retreats or training programs for committee leaders and members are appropriate times for such use.) Every pattern of sharing information affects: (1) the achievement of the goal of the group, (2) persons in the group, and (3) the organization of the group. Some patterns of information-sharing make it impossible for a group or organization to attain its goal. Other patterns make it difficult, but not impossible. One of the patterns in Exercise 5 (Group III) provides the potential for effective achievement but needs a leader and members who can work together. This pattern provides for the easiest flow of ideas, energy, skills and tools, but may need huge amounts of maintenance to keep it working effectively. It offers no panacea. The pattern presents only potential effectiveness. The willingness of persons to work on the goal in spite of individual and personality differences is a prerequisite for high-quality work. This warning note is sounded because there is a naive assumption that the buzz group is automatically the best pattern for sharing information. Its use may be disastrous if persons are not committed to the goal and to working with one another.

In the Group I pattern, the persons who are at the greatest distance will be isolated, tend to drop out of the group, and be least committed to the group and its goal. Group I easily becomes Group II if the person in the central position is an effective communicator and desires to control the group.

Group II is the most common pattern in the church, with the

church professional or committee chairperson in the central position. The pattern allows for easy manipulation by the person in the center. It takes an excessive amount of time to reach agreement, and the information overload on the central person is a particularly dangerous aspect of this pattern. Persons in the outer ring expect action, but the central person has to deal with competing and conflicting information from individuals and groups, so inactivity, even paralysis, is characteristic. Persons in the outer ring suspect that others are more influential on the person in the center. The pattern tends to produce problem solvers in the central position, but most of the problems in reality are between individuals and groups in the outer ring. Therefore, they are not amenable to the problem-solving efforts of the individual in the center. Frequently the person in the center internalizes the problem and is overwhelmed by the competition and conflict. What is essentially an organizational problem is personalized, and only personal solutions are forthcoming.

The Group II pattern is treated more extensively because it is so common and destructive. Church professionals tend to interpret ministry in terms of the individual and group relationships implied in this pattern. The effectiveness of a minister may be evaluated by the number of personal and group encounters the minister makes rather than by the health and effectiveness of the total congregation. Ministry is personalized by individual calls and attempts at individual problem-solving, while the needs of the congregation as a whole may be ignored. Clergy and other leaders are easily overwhelmed by problems in this pattern of sharing. When persons and groups withdraw their participation, when personal counseling is needed for professionals who discover they cannot solve all the problems, when a personal power base develops with selected members of the congregation, you have clear symptoms of the inadequacy of the information-sharing patterns in a congregation. Leaders get into personal trouble quickly when they can neither send nor receive the messages needed to maintain or increase their personal effectiveness. The pattern of information-sharing in a congregation influences the behavior of leaders and members.

The one-directional sharing of information in Groups V and VII patterns depends for even minimal effectiveness upon three things: member's loyalty to the leader, a system of effective rewards and punishments to maintain loyalty, and common goals by all parties and groups. The arrows in this pattern may deceive.

EXERCISE 5
INFORMATION-SHARING PATTERNS

Notes to leaders of this exercise.

1. Provide each participant a copy of Patterns of Information-Sharing.

2. If you have too few participants for seven groups, VII, VI, V and IV may be omitted in that order.

Purpose: To allow participants to experience the effects of different patterns of information-sharing on their own feelings of involvement, their attitudes toward the leader and other members of the group, and upon the group's ability to work toward its goal.

Method: Divide the participants into groups according to the diagrams on Patterns of Information-Sharing. Be sure that everyone understands that you may only speak to and hear from the person whose arrow touches your own circle.

Goal: To come to agreement in each group on an answer to the following question: What is the most significant problem confronting this congregation?

Procedure:

1. Organize the groups and have them quickly select their leader.

2. Allow forty minutes for the group to agree on an answer, communicating only as their respective pattern provides. Do not allow additional time.

3. Record on a blackboard or on newsprint:

    a. The leader's perception of the answer to the assigned question.
    b. The members' answer to the assigned question.

4. Discuss:

    a. Were all groups able to come to agreement?
    b. Do the leaders and the members agree on the answer?
    c. If not, how do you account for the difference?

5. Record how the participants felt about the leader, other members of the group, the task and the group's ability to work at it.

6. Discuss:

    a. The effects of the pattern upon the group's ability to work at its assignment.

    b. The effects of the pattern upon the involvement of the members.

    c. The effects of the pattern upon the leader.

    d. What are effective and ineffective ways of sharing information?

Patterns of Information-Sharing

Each circle represents a participant; each X represents a leader. Persons are allowed to *speak* to and *hear* only what is said by persons whose arrow touches their own circle.

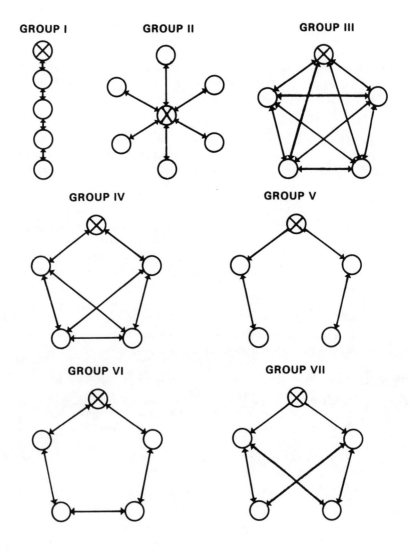

GROUP I   GROUP II   GROUP III

GROUP IV   GROUP V

GROUP VI   GROUP VII

They do not necessarily mean that there is no flow of information, although this may be true. They do mean that in spite of a steady flow of information, the leader does not hear or heed the information. In one large congregation with a Group V pattern of sharing information, the senior minister "purchased" loyalties through the provision of his summer home for his older associate minister, and promised regular salary increases for the younger assistant. The system of rewards in this congregation did not work. The older assistant was ready to retire to escape the developing turmoil in the congregation. The younger assistant was offended by the offer and moved as quickly as possible. The congregational frustration increased to the point where a commission of inquiry was established by the middle-level denominational organization. The commission of inquiry judged the situation to be intolerable for both the minister and the congregation, and recommended that before he accepted another position, the minister develop his capacity to listen and to obtain feedback from members of the congregation. The pattern of sharing did not allow either the senior minister or his assistants to obtain the necessary information from one another and the congregation. The professional staff in this congregation had diverse goals. They served different parts of the congregation so that each developed his own constituency. These different parts had diverse goals. Under these circumstances, the pattern of sharing information was grossly inadequate to maintain the effectiveness of the staff and the health of the congregation.

The Group VII pattern of sharing information tends to create rump groups and caucuses as quickly as though this were the intentional purpose of the leaders. In a sense this pattern invites organized responses by those who perceive they have goals for the congregation different from those of the leaders. When communication with leaders about goals is limited, members tend to organize to displace leaders and their goals.

The most profound effects of Groups V and VII patterns are on the leaders. They quickly sense isolation, persons plotting against them—whether real or imaginary—and a feeling of not being able to accomplish anything in the congregation. Feelings of anxiety quickly develop when adequate and accurate information does not inform leaders about the real conditions in the congregation. In lieu of accurate information, persons invent messages that may or may not be valid. These latter two patterns tend to produce leaders and leadership groups who are unable to lead and who become increasingly immobilized.

In the examination of patterns of information-sharing, a sympathetic understanding is required. Patterns of sharing develop over a period of time. They become institutionalized expectations of the ways in which leaders will behave, and ministers and lay leaders inherit these patterns unintentionally.

Most congregations have patterns of information-sharing that have been in use for years. These congregational patterns are a form of power affecting professionals, lay leaders, and members in unrecognized ways. In addition, they have profound consequences for goals and the health and effectiveness of the congregation.

Getting hold of the church and oneself in ministry and mission means creating the patterns of information-sharing that will promote health and effectiveness in the congregation and in leaders.

SUMMARY

In this discussion of the forms of power at work in a congregation, the implicit and unexamined nature of these forms has been emphasized. Power in its multiple expressions is at work affecting persons, their goals and the congregation as a living, human entity.

Few church professionals and lay members think organizationally. They do not see the effect that structures, political styles, polity, control of resources, and patterns of information-sharing have on persons, goals, and congregational behavior. They prefer individualistic solutions when trouble is sensed in a congregation. A few more pastoral calls are made to see if matters can be smoothed. Certain persons are not appointed to committees or elected to boards where they might be troublesome. Sermons are preached to individuals, urging love and reconciliation, but rarely justice in the church. Individuals and groups are isolated and ignored until they leave or organize to the extent they cannot be ignored. Then the pastor leaves or goes to a psychological clinic for rest and recuperation, or the district superintendent, the bishop, or the presbytery appoints an investigative committee to counsel with the minister and leaders. Both leaders and congregation feel guilty and repentant for a time. Then the conflict escalates again and the cycle repeats itself.

The pattern described above is far too prevalent to be explained away as due to defects in the personality of the minister or the laity. We have developed counseling services for the clergy on the assumption that there is "something wrong" with the minister. Or it is suggested that the congregation is "wrong" for him or her. True, sometimes that may be the case. But we should look at the organization as well as at individuals.

Organizational forms are powerful. They shape both church members and church professionals. In order to mobilize the church, we must think and act organizationally as well as individualistically. Professionals and laity must come to terms consciously and intentionally with the forms of power in a congregation and transform them so that goals, persons, and the congregation are cared for as an expression of Christian ministry.

CHAPTER 5

Environment:
Source of Anxiety and Promise

The environment of a congregation influences the policies and perspectives of persons as well as the goals, structure, polity, decision-making, and style of leadership of a congregation.

This chapter is written to enable professionals and laity to examine the ways in which environment influences a congregation. Three illustrations expose our lack of understanding of the impact of environment on the church.

1. During the decade following the Second World War practically all denominations located flegling congregations in thousands of new residential areas across the United States. Fifteen to twenty years and millions of dollars later, the painful process of selling the buildings and disbanding tiny congregations is taking place in hundreds, perhaps thousands, of these congregations which never grew much larger than the founding group.

2. Pastors who have been eminently effective in small-town churches are thought to be "eligible" to move up to larger urban and suburban congregations. Many who have done so discover quickly that the urban and suburban churches are not small-town congregations. The needs, tempo, interests, attitudes, and diversity of the two types of congregations are quite different. The minister attempts to do everything that made his or her ministry successful in the small-town church, only to discover that it doesn't accomplish the same results in the new congregation.

3. For a decade ministers and laypersons have been gathering in church meetings, speaking to one another, debating, and voting from a perspective that acknowledges the profound differences between the environments of cities, suburbs, and small towns. But our actions clearly demonstrate how little we understand of how

the church's ministry and mission are affected by differing environments. Different kinds of churches do not receive effective mutual support and assistance.

We have had a lack of clarity generally about the relationship between the environment and the behavior of an organization. In a stable environment in which the dominant religious, economic, political, and educational organizations did not change rapidly—medieval Europe, for instance—churches and other organizations could adapt slowly and without the obvious appearance of change. It was even possible to assume that the church was independent or autonomous in relation to environmental fluctuations. Only the historians remind us of the flip-flops of loyalties, policies, and programs, as the new regent was a Catholic queen in contrast to the previous Protestant king. But it does not take the historian to demonstrate the impact on local congregations of the civil rights movement, the women's liberation movement, the anti-war protests of the late '60s, nationalism in Asia and Africa, and a single increase in the price of oil in the Middle East. All have left their positive and negative marks on the church.

To assume that the church lives in a cocoon, safely shielded by its religious rhetoric and policies and procedures for excluding undesirable influences, is enormous self-deception. It also prevents the church from examining the environment and its impact on the church. To determine if a congregation is both adapting to and coping with the environment, there must be an examination of environmental impact. Most congregations are open systems. They experience the environment without impervious protective shields; and intentionally create policies and programs to respond to the environment. Some congregations, however, attempt to construct protective insulators. But over a period of time few are successful.

The uncertainty that a diverse and rapidly changing environment such as ours introduces into church organization can be responded to only when we conclude that the church is in a dynamic relation to its environment. Therefore, intentional and positive efforts must be made to develop appropriate responses of ministry and mission. Two environmental factors, recession and inflation, will be disastrous for hundreds of congregations. Most of these congregations will be forced to examine alternatives by direction of an external body: the conference, synod, diocese, or presbytery. The issue is not whether the environment is influencing the church, but whether a congregation is developing goals, policies, and programs that will enable it to cope effectively with its environment. Many congregations are influenced by the environment to such an extent that their capacity to adapt and respond to new conditions is depleted before they are aware that death as a congregation is imminent.

In this chapter we will look generally at the relationship between environmental factors and behaviors of a congregation. We will then proceed to examine more carefully how environmental influences make their way into congregational life as information from the environment. The role of procedures for recruiting and incorporating new members in bringing environmental influences into the congregation will be studied next. Finally, a brief section will focus on the meaning of environmental influences for the development of policies and programs by congregational leaders.

ENVIRONMENT AND CONGREGATIONAL LIFE

The word "congregation" causes most persons to think immediately of the Sunday morning worship service. Few persons will have an image of committees, programs, projects, or the church school. Nor will they think of the select group of persons who attend worship services in contrast to the majority of members who stay away from Sunday services. The common imagery suggests also that the Sunday morning service is the primary influence in the congregation. If conditions of apathy or tension arise, first examine the sermon and liturgy. While the sermon and liturgy are certainly important, their dominant image prevents persons from seeing the more complex forces at work there. Centuries of terrible preaching and formal liturgies, even in foreign tongues, have not killed the church in stable or slowly changing environments.

Rapidly changing environments have their impact on every aspect of congregational life. New goals for church life arise. Members of congregations reflect their desires for a different quality of life in the congregation, for action rather than passivity. They want small study groups rather than entertaining programs for large groups, a variety of programming rather than a standardized denominational package, new caring ministries by members for members rather than professional care. Some members even perceive that they are cared for when they are allowed to develop a church-community project.

Changing environments also mean new directions in church-community ministry. During the past twenty years congregations have become involved in dramatically new forms of community ministries as new environments have called forth new responses. The rapidly changing emphasis points to the impact of rapidly changing environments. New issues have arisen in congregations that had no awareness of the environmental forces behind them. Divisiveness and paralysis have resulted as members have debated the question of what are appropriate goals for the congregation in the community.

The change of the name from Foreign Missions to Ecumenical Mission meant a fundamental shift of goals in relation to the world. Nationalism in Asia and Africa, the increase in industrialism, the rise in educational levels of nations (all of which are impressive signs of the success of Foreign Missions), meant a shift from mission on our terms to missions on the basis of their goals. Congregations and denominations are split between those who desire to continue supporting missionaries in the old Foreign Missions pattern and those who are committed to work with and support the new National Churches of Central and South America, Asia, and Africa. The pattern of no goals for a congregation's involvement in world mission is also seen. Increasingly as the vision has blurred of sending missionaries to do good in distant lands, there is more ambiguity and "goallessness" in relation to the larger world. The goals of a congregation are influenced directly by both the environment of a local community and the environment of a nation and the world.

Environments influence total congregational assets as well as goals. The movement of a major industry in or out of a community affects the ideas, money, and number of persons available. Some industries—i.e., electronics, research and development, engineering—junior colleges, and new universities bring with them educated, sophisticated leadership with cosmopolitan backgrounds. Other industries, such as meat-packing, paper mills, poultry, hosiery, bring skilled technicians and workers who are primarily local in background with only a small educated management group. Sometimes small-town churches are hit hard by the practices of large chain stores that move local store managers frequently, particularly when these persons are a source of new ideas, energy, and money.

Sophisticated, cosmopolitan communities bring new methods of teaching, accounting, and leadership into a congregation. Members of congregations in these communities are not surprised by new technologies in the church. Parents tend to expect and support contemporary educational technologies: simulation games, programmed instruction, closed circuit television, etc. Congregations in more stable, isolated communities do not have the same methods and technologies in their environments. They do not expect to find them in the church.

Leadership styles appear to be more or less effective in the environment in which they are learned. The small-town, informal style of decision-making and leadership is quite different from the technical planning, teamwork, or committee problem-solving style of modern industry. One group has technical tools, and can aggressively tackle congregational problems. The other group can informally work with local influential persons to raise the budget, repair church buildings, and solve personal problems in the congregation and community. Each group gives a congregation different capacities to work on goals in relation to the environment, community, and larger world. The environment of a congregation directly influences the kind and number of leaders available to it. Leadership in a congregation reflects either the leadership style of the larger community or the effectiveness of current congregational leaders in limiting or excluding other styles of leadership. In many congregations there is conflict between old-time community residents with the informal style of decision-making and the new, aggressive members who have different ideas on how to run the church. Professionals tend to identify with one or the other group, depending upon their personal goals and their personal goals for the church, and on their perception of the relative power of the two groups. The environment surrounding a congregation provides leaders with distinctive styles and capacities. The congregation through its internal personnel practices, nominating committees, committee appointment practices, etc., either incorporates persons into the leadership of the congregation or excludes them. Either way, the capacity of the congregation to achieve its goals is affected.

Organizations tend to reflect the characteristics of the dominant environment around them. This is true of congregations as well as small businesses, banks, schools, and industry. The structure, rules and procedures (even when prescribed by a larger denominational body), decision-making processes, climate and patterns of communication reflect the characteristics found in the businesses and industry of the community. The dominant characteristics are rarely challenged except when a new minister or associate is em-

ployed and brings ideas and commitment to different organizational characteristics, or when an industry moves into a community bringing personnel who are committed to different organizational methods. Suburban churches, which had been small-town
congregations before the population explosion, drew leadership
primarily from the town. Later the numbers of new residents from
industries with extensive management-training programs overwhelmed them. Ministers have been caught between the two
competing and conflicting groups. The new residents tend to
bring different personal goals and different personal goals for the
congregation. The existing congregational characteristics did not
and do not now, in many instances, have the capacity to allow a
congregation to deal effectively with such diversity. Rapidly
changing environments present possible new organizational characteristics. Congregational leaders incorporate or reject the organizational characteristics of the surrounding environment.

Communities also provide persons for potential incorporation
into congregational life. Every community can be characterized
by the kinds and numbers of persons residing in it. This is obvious.
Census tracts have contained this information for years, but leaders of most congregations have yet to look at the meaning of this
information for congregational life or, more important, at the
ways in which the congregation has responded to particular
groups in the community. Most congregations look at growth in
numbers as their most important goal. Yet some congregations
exist in communities that have ceased to grow, and are actually
declining in numbers. These communities generally experience
an early depletion of single young adults, young couples, and aggressive community leaders. The congregations and their pastor
are under terrible psychological pressure to grow, when realistically growth is *not* possible. Congregations are not allowed to
recognize the futility of this goal and to focus their available resources and commitments on more realistic goals. Denominational
agencies and regional denominational units push growth in numbers when the only moral option is to focus on goals of ministry
and mission which are achievable and important to the particular
congregation in its community. The pressure to grow, on the one
hand, and the steady decrease in the size of the community, on the
other, produce apathy and low morale in congregations and pastors. Denominational leaders invariably bring "successful" pastors
from exceptionally rapid growth communities to encourage dis-
pirited pastors in declining communities. This insensitivity and

callousness to the plight of the pastor and the effect of environment upon pastors and congregations is inexcusable. There are
communities that experience rapid growth of particular age
groups—young couples, single young adults, families with teenag-
ers, or older couples whose children are grown. These persons
bring special challenges and opportunities for congregations.
When persons with different expectations, skills, attitudes, and
knowledge enter a community, and consequently a congregation,
it is always in order to ask: How appropriate for them is the present program, ministry, and mission?

New persons in a community can evoke at least two kinds of
responses from a congregation. One characteristic response is to
seal off the congregation from the new persons and their influences. There are a variety of sealing-off activities. Governing
boards fence in the church parking lot and lock the gates to pre-
vent neighborhood youth from playing basketball. Whole neigh-
borhoods in close proximity to the church are ignored as new
ethnic, racial, or social class groups move into these neighbor-
hoods. Internally, new residents may be encouraged to attend
church and teach in the church school, if the congregation is
desperate for teachers. Otherwise, persons may have to attend
church for years before they are noticed and become eligible for
election to an office. Some congregations have written rules re-
quiring persons to be members for five to ten years before they
may serve on a governing board. Other congregations have tacit
agreements to serve the same end. Persons who may be exceptionally large contributors to the church, those who occupy a status
position in a local business or industry, and persons who have
attitudes and values similar to the minister's will most easily break
through the sealing-off procedures. Unless congregational leaders
see new environmental influences as a positive good, they will
most likely attempt to seal off the congregation. Sealing off is
never completely effective in a turbulent environment. Few congregations have been able to seal off or ignore the impact of the
high school drug culture on the church youth group. Many congregations have lost their ministry to youth because they thought the
drug culture could be ignored. The high school with its culture
was not seen as a legitimate target for ministry. Resources of the
community were not mobilized for ministry with adolescents.

Sealing-off activities appear to work for brief periods of time,
but over longer periods environmental forces work incessantly to
produce their impact. Too, sealing-off activities rarely mobilize a

congregation for ministry and mission in the face of new challenges. Rather, they become the rules and procedures developed by leaders of a congregation to keep out what they perceive as threatening influences. These rules and procedures do not activate persons and groups to develop the most appropriate and effective responses.

Coping activities, on the other hand, are designed to call forth the resources of a congregation to meet challenges as effectively as possible. Rather than building a fence around the church parking lot, a congregation discovers within it persons to develop a ministry with youth. Or it reallocates funds from its budget to employ a person part time to develop the church's youth ministry, using the available resources of the congregation.

In communities where new ethnic, racial, or social classes are attempting to develop a satisfying life, congregations may sponsor cooperative buying clubs, language classes, medical and legal clinics, alternative education for children and young people. In the nineteenth century, congregations provided these ministries to persons on other continents. These were deemed highly spiritual and appropriate activities for persons thousands of miles away. They are equally spiritual and appropriate coping activities for congregations and communities with diverse populations immediately surrounding them.

It is obvious that there is disagreement as to what constitutes sealing-off and coping activities. Congregational life in our environment is such that diverse groups see actions, programs, rules, and procedures quite differently. No congregation or congregational leaders have sufficient knowledge about constituents. Personal goals and personal goals for the congregation are relatively unknown. Hunches and guesses are poor substitutes for processes in which members can make this information available in their own language, and in relation to current congregational goals. Congregational leaders generally see members in terms of current congregational goals rather than in terms of their potential capacity to serve new goals that would enable the congregation to cope more effectively with its environment.

Sealing-off and coping activities are developed through committees, projects, and programs, and are structurally lodged in parts of the congregation. These parts are used to seal off influences or to cope with different aspects of the environment. This arrangement means that different groups in the congregation relate to different challenges and influences in the environment. The congregation as a whole does not experience the environment in the same way. Differential experiences of the environment build different commitments, interests, attitudes, and personal goals for the congregation. Competition and conflict develop between persons in these different parts, and leaders, consequently, tend to seal off troublesome areas. Congregational leaders generally attempt to seal off the parts that are exposed to the most troublesome, disruptive aspects of the environment. These areas, while troublesome and difficult to manage for a minority elite group, may in the long run provide the most effective actions and programs for coping with the environment. Most of the tension organizationally is between parts that are influenced most by history and tradition and those which are affected most by the environment.

The environment produces for congregations new conditions that necessitate coping or sealing-off activities. No congregation can remain neutral in its environment; it must deal with it negatively or positively. An understanding of the effects of the environment on a congregation, its members and parts, is essential for wise rule and effective management.

THE INFLUENCE OF INFORMATION FROM THE ENVIRONMENT

Information from the environment influences congregational life through persons and groups. But leaders and leadership groups that lack categories for seeing and understanding how information makes its way into congregational life, and that are insensitive to messages of persons and groups, might perceive that a congregation is in turmoil, yet not understand the sources of the turmoil and not develop adequate processes for looking at the messages. Too frequently, leaders view persons and groups as troublemakers without making an effort to understand the messages and their sources in the environment.

William R. Dill, in his article "The Impact of Environment on Organizational Development,"[15] suggests several categories that are useful in studying the input from persons and groups. Dill suggests looking at information apart from persons and groups. It is more helpful for understanding the church to see information as connected with persons and groups in order to appreciate its meaning and force. These categories assist groups in understanding some of the processes and environmental influences at work in a congregation.

1. Some persons and groups serve as *triggers to action.* Their function is to arouse the consciousness of the congregation's leaders until they become increasingly aware of events and conditions in the surrounding environment. These persons want leaders and the congregation to act, to shift resources, to begin new programs and projects. Leaders are generally aware of the names of persons and groups that are most effective in triggering action in a congregation. These persons tend to be dissatisfied with the current state of affairs and press for more adequate and appropriate policies, programs, and projects.

2. Persons and groups also provide *information about goals.* These persons are a reservoir of concerns and commitment which may be expressed directly and clearly, or indirectly and vaguely. Most members have never stated their goals, but join a congregation and participate on the basis of an unstated perception of the congregation's purposes and directions. This perception may be accurate or inaccurate. But such persons bring from the environment outside the congregation experiences that are frequently formulated in a vague sense of purpose and direction for the congregation.

One of the major strategies for changing congregations in the past decade has been to gather information about a congregation's environment as the basis for goal formulation. Questionnaires, surveys, interpretation of census tracts, have been used to compile a picture of a community. Either blue-ribbon committees of congregations have been appointed to conduct the study and develop recommendations, or an external "expert" has been employed to do the same for the leadership group. Several assumptions lie behind this strategy. First, it is assumed that surveys, census tracts, and questionnaires will yield information that will have power to mobilize leaders and a congregation. Second, a power is given to information, data, so-called facts, which this information does not have apart from persons and groups. Leaders of congregations have conducted hundreds of studies, summarized, interpreted the information, and developed recommendations. In most instances little implementation has been achieved. In congregations where there are diverse persons and groups with information about goals, formal leaders may not be trusted to conduct studies and develop recommendations for the congregation.

Leaders and congregations are most able to deal effectively with information about goals when that information is connected di-

rectly to persons and groups. These persons and groups can interpret their information about the environment and suggest goals
they think are appropriate responses to the environment. Studies
conducted through questionnaires and surveys by persons external to the congregation are not able to show leaders the relationship between the intensity and extensiveness of feelings and perceptions. These latter characteristics are part of the needed
information about goals. They reveal the actual nature and potential of the congregation. They suggest how many persons are committed to particular goals, and how deeply.

If there are *no* legitimate ways for persons and groups to share
information about goals, informal and illegitimate processes will
be developed. If these latter are not effective and eventually made
legitimate, then persons tend to create political processes to gain
a new set of leaders or to drop out.

Very little attention has been given to ways in which leaders of
congregations handle information about goals. Most leaders have
not developed legitimate and routine ways for members to share
such information. Rather, they tend to listen only after a crisis has
developed, and then they may listen defensively. These same
leaders are frequently bewildered and astonished when persons
do not trust them to act on information. As persons and groups
perceive, correctly or incorrectly, that leaders do not deal justly
with their information about goals, they demand increasingly explicit actions from leaders to prove they can be trusted. A vicious
cycle results in which minister(s) and members frequently leave
the congregation or wish they could leave. The prevalence of
ministers desiring to leave their present congregations, and of
members who are apathetic or withholding their personal commitment is, probably, much greater than presently imagined. A
turbulent environment produces persons with diverse information about the goals of a congregation. Unless clergy and lay leaders can develop legitimate and routine processes for sharing and
acting on this information, not much of significance will happen
in the church.

3. Not all the present troubles of the church are due to inadequate processes for dealing with information about goals or to
leaders who do not want to listen. Until recently little attention
has been given to gathering *information about the means to
achieve goals*. Congregations may have excellent leaders who
have listened and adopted appropriate goals. But they may dis-

cover they have empty statements of goals because they do not know how to achieve them. Diverse populations and diverse goals are not always amenable to the traditional means of achievement. Not all high school age young people are helped through the traditional ministry of the church school class, Christian Endeavor, or youth fellowships created in particular moments of history with an environment and an understanding of Christian faith that called for such a response. Hospitals and schools as an expression of Christian faith were effective means to achieve a goal of ministry in another moment. Many congregations are distressed by their present ineffectiveness in preparing young people for church membership. Memorizing traditional catechisms or attending the traditional confirmation class does not appear to be an effective means for incorporating young persons into the life of the church. Appropriate goals and effective means to achieve congregational goals are both necessary.

Congregational leaders must be much more intentional about searching for appropriate means to achieve congregational goals. Few persons are actually involved in providing information of any kind to leaders. The fact that the names of certain persons and groups appear repeatedly shows the limited sources of information available to leaders to inform their judgments and planning. In most congregations there are only a few persons who provide information in a systematic, recognizable manner.

Positive involvement and the morale of a congregation increase not only with a statement of goals, representing the interest and commitments of members, but with effective achievement of them.

The environment surrounding a congregation contains information about the ways goals can be achieved as well as information about goals. This information can be "captured" through legitimate formal processes designed by leaders.

4. Every congregation has its persons and groups that supply *information about constraints* at work in the congregation. These persons and groups can tell leaders why a program or project will not work, or why persons will not cooperate when the schedule is changed for the church school or for Sunday morning worship. They are sources of both accurate and inaccurate information about how persons in the congregation and community feel about real or projected changes. They interpret community sentiment about the church and its activities. These persons tend to set limits

on various aspects of congregational life on the basis of their perception of reality.

These persons and groups are perceived ambiguously in most
congregations. To some leaders and members, they are "enemies." To others, they are allies, the first to be consulted, and they
can veto almost any projected change. If these persons or groups
are members of status groups, they may wield enormous power to
frustrate ministers, leaders, and groups in the congregation.

Information about constraints is important when it is accurate.
Planning goal implementation and achievement is enhanced by
information about constraints. Leaders and congregations experience trouble when the information is inaccurate, or when a minority is effective in thwarting projected congregational activities and
projects through the sharing of such information.

Leaders of congregations need accurate information about constraints, and they need persons and groups who provide such
information. These persons and groups relate to different aspects
of the environment. They are important to the life of the congregation. But there is need for accurate and open perceptions of
such persons and groups so that their information can be verified
and made available to leaders and the congregation.

5. Most congregations have persons and groups that provide
evaluation and judgments on congregational performance. This
information represents valuable feedback to leaders and the congregation about its performance in relation to its purposes. For the
most part this information is not sought from members of the
congregation or community, but it is provided informally and
gratuitously outside the formal channels of communication. Since
there are few legitimate ways for receiving such information,
there are few, if any, effective ways for responding to these evaluations and judgments. Ministers and lay leaders hear this type of
information in informal settings, where there are no institutional
mechanisms for response. The only possible response is personal,
and therefore usually unsatisfactory. Organizational channels are
needed to respond to evaluations and judgments about and from
the congregation rather than pastors and a few lay leaders responding personally. The appropriate response to negative
evaluations may be a congregational action, project, or program
which is designed to meet an environmental challenge. This may
be a different program for confirmation, a day care center for the

children of working mothers, an extensive ministry with the elderly, or a folk worship service at 6:00 P.M. on Saturday evenings.

Evaluations and judgments about congregational performance need to be regularized as part of the total congregational life. The congregation needs to look at itself and make decisions on the basis of what it sees. Leaders need to design and implement such processes so that they have the necessary information for wise rule. Otherwise ministers and leaders interpret evaluation personally, and give personal responses. Personal responses can never be satisfactory when the congregation or some aspect of congregational life is the problem.

Need for Formal Processes of Information-Gathering A major problem in the church is that information comes from too few people in an informal, irregular manner. Consequently, leaders do not have accurate information about the congregation. Information cannot be separated from persons and groups if the meaning, intensity, and power of this information is to be understood. Formal, legitimate processes for gathering various types of information from a congregation are needed. If they do not exist, informal channels will be created continually to carry the concerns and commitments of persons and groups. Informal channels that lie outside the regular congregational processes cannot be managed by leaders for the health and benefit of the congregation. Nor can there be a congregational response to environmental challenges if there is only personal, informal sharing of information. Congregational resources cannot be mobilized when needed information is located in a few individuals and groups.

NEW MEMBERS: A MIXED BLESSING

There is enormous pressure on every congregation to keep membership rolls growing. Ministers and congregations gain status if a congregation grows rapidly. Status generally means more power and influence in denominational and other church circles. New members mean there are more persons to pay bills, an assistant or associate can be employed, buildings can be repaired, and new equipment can be purchased. Growth is good and Christian because it implements that mandate to "save souls," "to make disciples of all nations," "to evangelize." There are numerous and, at least some, good reasons to increase the size of congregations.

But growth can also be destructive of a congregation and of effective ministry and mission.

The unmanageable character of many congregations is due to an increase in membership without adequate recruitment and incorporation procedures. In "Latent Culture: A Note on the Theory of Latent Social Roles," Becker and Geer introduce the concepts of "manifest" and "latent" cultures in human organizations.[16] These concepts are helpful in understanding another aspect of the relationship between the environment and congregational life. The recruitment of new members is another way in which information from the environment makes its way into a congregation. The more transient and diverse a community, the greater the possibility of new influences from the environment as new members join the church.

Each congregation has a culture, a set of perspectives on the different areas of congregational life, such as mission, maintenance of the congregation, and social life. This set of perspectives is experienced and it influences persons as it is manifest in a congregation. Each congregation, therefore, has a "manifest culture."

The significance of manifest culture is that it is the source of the most consistent and persistent information available to persons. It is experienced through all of the senses and, consequently, is the most powerful instrument of teaching. It is more powerful than preaching, because it provides the context for preaching and it interprets the sermons. The set of perspectives manifest in a congregation influences the style and content of sermons, the language of the preacher, the type of illustrations, etc. If a preacher cannot preach in a manner consistent with the set of perspectives that is manifest in a congregation, he or she is in trouble. Congregations, if they are not goalless, express their perspectives on mission, on maintenance of congregational life, and on social life or fellowship, in multiple ways. Programs, activities, church announcements in bulletins and newspapers, agendas of meetings, budgeting of money and time of clergy and members—every aspect of church life teaches and affects the attitudes and perspectives of persons who relate in various ways to the congregation. The manifest culture is not generally challenged in a congregation that is in a stable community, and in which there is not a significant increase in new members. New members and a changing community provide the seeds for challenging the manifest culture. Congregations that are in a changing community and that gain new members quickly are likely to have a dominant manifest culture, and a latent culture waiting to sprout under optimum conditions.

A "latent culture" is a set of perspectives on congregational life that lie dormant until an event or crisis evokes them in a manifest form. They are dormant in persons and groups until they are activated by other persons and events.

As new members join a congregation, they may bring in a very different set of perspectives on congregational life than is currently manifest. Mission in the congregation may be currently defined as increasing church membership. New members may desire to send missionaries from the congregation to Asia or Africa. Another group of new members may desire that the congregation sponsor a community organization, a day care center, a halfway house for former prisoners, or a ministry to drug addicts as the mission of the congregation.

The congregation may have a quality adult education program, but new members may desire only social programs. Or there may be a women's association with excellent study and important projects for women, but the new women members may desire programs for couples, or a more activist-oriented program for women committed to women's liberation. Congregational life in the future can be anticipated as the latent culture of the present is formed and identified. Latent cultures exist to be activated under new conditions. New members activate old members who already have—lying dormant—similar interests and commitments. Many congregations are arenas of a dynamic flowing of ideas, attitudes, and expectations between old and potentially new cultures. Most leaders are aware of the teeming activity, but are unaware of its sources and how the congregation can be managed more effectively.

Congregational self-understanding of its purposes and directions is the crucial aspect of management. When a congregation has self-identity, that is, when it knows what it is doing as a congregation, leaders can create recruitment and incorporation processes for new members which affirm and support these purposes. Or they may intentionally and regularly develop new possible directions for the congregation by identifying the interests and commitments of new members and providing possibilities for them to act upon their commitments. New members will act on their commitments. They will act through apathy, or agitation, through acquiescing momentarily to the manifest culture and waiting for the moment to implement their commitments, or through understanding the strengths and weaknesses of the present culture and contributing via formal channels their own perspective for strengthening the congregation's witness.

Recruitment and incorporation processes of a congregation influence most directly the development of latent cultures. These processes can be described as either "discriminate" or "indiscriminate." Discriminate processes are discrete and purposeful. They have definite form and their effectiveness in achieving the purposes assigned to them can be evaluated. Indiscriminate processes, on the other hand, are without clear purposes. They lack definite form, and there is little clarity about the results expected from such processes. (See Figure 6.)

Rapid growth in congregations results in latent cultures that are continually becoming manifest. The typical recruitment process enables a prospective member to become a member with a minimum knowledge of the purposes, significance, and projected future directions of the congregation. Leaders and current members learn little of the interests and commitment of prospective members. New members are not actively incorporated into the life of the congregation to assist in achieving its purposes.

New members are voted into membership by rump groups of governing boards in the church foyers. They are, in some congregations, given a tour of the building, a lecture on the significance and uniqueness of the denomination, and the rules and procedures (polity) of the local congregation. In others, instruction on the Confession of Faith is provided. Few attempts are made to acquaint prospective members with the character, nature, and directions of the congregation they are joining. The intent of most leaders, it appears, is to receive persons as rapidly as possible with little thought as to how the entry of persons can be most effectively achieved. The possible future consequences for persons or congregation that accepts such indiscriminate processes is given little attention.

Many current problems in congregational life are due to lack of care and thoughtfulness in recruiting and incorporating new members. Exclusion on the basis of social class, race, or ethnic background is not morally permissible in the church, and this is not written to suggest such discrimination. But it does suggest that the interests of the congregation and the new members be cared for in ways that do justice both to currently existing perspectives and to the new perspectives which members may bring as they join. Discriminate processes make it possible to develop ways in-

FIGURE 6
CHARACTERISTICS OF RECRUITMENT
AND INCORPORATION PROCESSES

RECRUITMENT

Discriminate	Indiscriminate
Clear effort is made to interpret congregation's goals and program to prospective member.	No effort is made to interpret congregation's goals and program to prospective member.
Effort is made to learn prospective member's expectations in becoming a member.	Expectations of prospective member are not sought.
Members of the congregation have a part in recruiting new members and interpreting its programs and activities to them.	Only the minister and elected officers deal with prospective members.
Each step of the recruiting process and its purpose is made clear.	Let it be known that anyone interested will be welcome.
Interests, experience, skills, and motive of prospective members are considered.	No effort is made to discover the interests, skills, experience, and motive of prospective members.
Decision that membership will be mutually beneficial is made by leaders and prospective members.	Leaders of church accept for membership anyone who expresses interest.

INCORPORATION

Discriminate	Indiscriminate
Efforts are made to involve new members in programs and activities according to their needs and interests.	New members are allowed to drift after joining church.
Regular processes to review new member's participation and progress are followed.	No clear processes exist to review participation and progress of new members.
Skill, interest, and experience are taken into account in assigning responsibility.	Many new members become inactive because no effort is made to discover skills and interest.
Criticism, proposals, and new ideas are sought from new members.	No procedures exist for follow-up on new members.

tentionally for persons of diverse interests and commitments to participate effectively in a purposeful congregation.

ENVIRONMENT AND LEADERSHIP OF CONGREGATIONS

In too many congregations there is an assumption that the church is the minister's, and many ministers confirm this assumption with their actions. If there is apathy, low morale, tension between persons and groups, lack of purpose and direction, it is assumed that the minister is responsible, and sometimes the cause of these conditions. The minister may or may not be responsible for some of the conditions found in a congregation. But it should be apparent that congregations are complex institutions existing in a dynamic relationship to their environment. They are not solely the products of the adequacy or inadequacy of professional leaders.

Congregations have profound transactions with the environment. Goals, structure, polity, political activity, and leadership are affected by these transactions. The last chapter will deal with these topics at greater length. Here let us emphasize that goals, organization, procedures, decision-making, and leadership are challenged and influenced by different environments. Congregations in placid, stable communities receive different information from those where there is more turbulence. The leadership needs of congregations differ in each type of environment. Some readers will argue that there are no stable environments, and consequently the leadership needs are the same. To some extent, this may be so. Still, environments differ in degrees of turbulence, and whatever the environmental condition, the state of the congregation is not solely the professional's responsibility.

Leadership groups must take responsibility for the nature and direction of congregational life. Ultimately they must lead in such a manner that the congregation is encouraged to take responsibility for its own character and purpose. It is not morally or theologically responsible to suggest that the minister is the congregation, or even that the governing board is the congregation. The congregation is a diverse mixture of interests and commitments that reflect the involvements and concerns of participation in the larger community.

This means that leadership is not just charismatic or expressive. Neither is it only ritualistic and symbolic. Effective leadership is instrumental, managerial, and congregationally oriented. It recognizes that there is a human organization, a congregation, which needs leaders who will work for the health, effectiveness, and character of the whole congregation.

The environment poses fundamental policy concerns for leaders and congregations. Most congregations are now experiencing environments that tend to dispense or reject particular programs and activities. Women's associations, men's organizations, Sunday church school for adults, and employed choirs are illustrations of activities that are challenged and rejected in many environments.

Other congregations are experiencing the need to shift to different church school curricular resources, new confirmation class materials, new mission programs in the community, and new ways of caring for church members. Decisions as to the appropriate time to shift, which resources to choose, which goals to pursue that will allow the congregation to respond effectively are policy decisions that changing environment necessitates.

Still other congregations are composed of such diverse groups that there is no longer substantial agreement even on the direction and purposes of the congregation. Leaders and congregations then need to develop agreement on goals and the means to achieve them.

There are some congregations in which there is agreement on goals but no agreement on the means to achieve them. Leadership, then, must seek to educate or influence the diverse groups in the congregation to accept or modify current projects, programs, and activities. Evangelism and social action are areas of congregational life in which there is substantial agreement on the abstract goal, but wide divergence on the means to achieve the goal.

The above illustrations represent policy concerns of leaders and congregations which an environment may impose, and which need policy formulation by leaders.

Most congregational leaders fail to deal with the impact of environmental influences except as crises arise which demand attention. For the most part, meetings of governing boards are ritualistic. There is little systematic examination of environmental influences, little policy formulation to deal with long-range issues. Policies are formed primarily by inaction. Committees and groups form policy for the congregation only as they respond to particular crises, needs, and challenges. Governing boards are seldom involved in policy formulation, nor do they involve congregations in such activity. But leaders need to be involved in policy formulation. The congregation must have purposes or goals and clear processes by which they are to be achieved. Critical reflection on the quality and character of such goals and the processes used to attain them are the most significant areas of leadership activity.

Policies are also required in relation to the forms of congregational power, and how this power is to be used most effectively to achieve congregational goals. The nature and use of power includes a concern for the direction, amount, and processes of distribution of congregational resources. It is a legitimate sphere of policy formation.

The structure and development of congregational life is yet another area that needs policy formation. The nature, character, direction, and purposes of congregational life need intentional reflection and policies that will guide a congregation toward a particular future that is expressive of the theological commitments of the congregation.

Finally, leaders need to be involved in policy formation which affects the motivation of members. Motivation is strongly influenced by the policies and leadership styles of leaders. Behavior of the congregation is influenced in numerous ways, negatively and positively, by leadership groups. What do leaders and leadership groups intend the quality of life within a congregation to be? What policies do they propose as appropriate to enable a congregation to attain a particular quality of life? What particular programs in relation to a community do they envision?

The meetings of governing boards in many congregations are conducted with the same items on the agenda, in the same order as they had fifteen to twenty years ago. Important current concerns do not always get first priority. They may even be omitted, because they cause controversy. Routine business tends to drive out creative thinking and planning. Individual members or groups may hold a disproportionate amount of power to shape the agenda, and consequently the goals of the congregation.

In order to respond more effectively to environmental challenges, a new style of leadership is needed. It is a style that actively seeks to understand environmental influences and to mobilize the resources of the congregation to respond. This means that leaders must assist congregations to agree on priority goals. More must be known about the resources of a congregation, including the kind of resources available and the amount. Then policies must be developed to achieve priority goals by focusing available resources upon them. Other goals, programs, projects, and activities may be subordinated so that priority goals are achieved.

All this implies that leaders must plan, and make choices to achieve a plan. There is not much history of this kind of leadership in the church, but there is evidence that both laity and clergy have the intelligence and desire to provide such leadership when the perspective, tools, and skills are made available. Turbulent environments create new demands upon leaders. Congregations need new policies, new coalitions, and fresh mobilization of congregational resources. Getting hold of the church and ministry is a practical activity, which needs to be informed and guided by Christian faith. We turn now to Chapter 6 to look at one way in which Christian faith can be related to such practical activity.

CHAPTER 6

Thinking About
the Church and Ministry

We have looked at the church in terms of the interaction between personal goals, personal goals for the congregation, congregational goals, forms of power and their effect on the involvement of persons, and the ways in which the environment makes its way into congregational life. When passions and personalities are added as other forces at work, the congregation becomes truly a gathering of strangers capable of producing identity crises in any and all its members. Congregations are not just clergy, leaders, and members in some aggregate, amorphous form. Congregations are composed of dynamic patterns of relationships and purposes that regulate and govern persons. Clergy and laity are, to a great extent, unaware of the full extent of this regulation and its meaning and impact on persons.

Congregations also have a history and a culture in which the history is embedded. This culture contains not only congregational beliefs, but also patterns of relationship between clergy and laity, leaders and clergy, and leaders and members of a congregation. Leadership styles have been transmitted from one generation of leaders to another through a congregation's culture. This means that leadership, as an activity, has often escaped critical reflection. Leaders in many congregations govern unreflectively, protecting their interests, doing what they think best for the congregation, perpetuating structures and goals, and using the various forms of power (quite unwittingly much of the time) to manage the congregation. Remarkably little attention has been given to the church itself. We have taken for granted the church as an institution, assuming that Christian leadership takes place when meetings of governing boards open with prayer and Bible-reading, and when occasionally time is allotted in meetings for discussion of a chapter of a book with a Christian theme. These are important uses of the resources of Christian faith in preparation for leadership. But engaging in these activities is not the same thing as Christian leadership. Nor is it clear how these traditional activities will enable leaders to involve diverse members and groups in the church and its ministry. Leaders and members need additional tools, and methods for using the tools, to enable them to get on with the work the church is appointed to do.

A critical problem for leaders and members to ponder is the relationship between theory (theology) and the practice of ministry. Karl Rahner has emphasized this need as he suggests two features that should characterize pastoral or practical theology:

> First, it is not confined exclusively to the work of clergy or to the "cure of souls" exercised by these in the narrower sense of the term. Rather it extends to everything with which the Church as such has to do, beginning from the worldwide Church and extending right down to local churches and the individual communities of believers. . . .
>
> The second characteristic of a pastoral theology . . . consists in the fact that an exact scientific investigation must be made into the concrete situation of the church both interior and exterior, since in practice the achievement of her own fulness depends upon this. Moreover this investigation must be conducted in a theological manner since while the analysis of the contemporary situation does in deed presuppose the findings of the secular sciences, still for the purposes of pastoral theology it must be conducted in a specifically theological way.[17]

Much has been written about our current crisis of faith. The impact of science and secularism upon persons has received much attention and speculation by theologians, but practical theology has received almost no attention. A central point in this book is that the problem for clergy and laity is not just secularism and science, but the church itself: its purposes, nature, relationships, and vitality. The socially *real* church is troublesome to clergy and laity. The church as a concrete, social, and historical reality is the first hurdle for both ministers and lay persons. It needs a practical theology that enables church people to deal with the church as it is and with the relationships between church and community.

It is not possible at this time to write *a* practical theology, nor is it desirable to write one. *Doing* practical theology is a more hopeful and appropriate way to inquire about common life in the church. There are some guidelines that can be suggested for the doing of practical theology. These have been sifted from the various writings of Dietrich Bonhoeffer and from one important essay written by Jürgen Moltmann which summarizes the various themes about which Bonhoeffer writes on the Lordship of Christ.[18]

Four elements in Bonhoeffer's writings seem important for the doing of practical theology about God's reign in the church and community:

1. There is need to look at the intent of Christian doctrine to discover the full significance of Christian faith for the church. Particularly, the social intent should be discovered and applied to social and institutional activities and realities.

2. Congregational life is one location where the authentic personhood of both clergy and laity is formed, reformed, and expressed.

3. Congregations are more than shapeless collections of individuals. They have a spirit, a character of their own.

4. God's reign is expressed in both social and ethical activity in places where authentic personhood is being shaped and where the spirit of the larger, social-institutional entity is affecting the spirit of persons.

Bonhoeffer challenges the traditional doctrines about Christian faith which have, he claims, been interpreted individualistically. Theology and the doctrines that summarize theology were ideas traditionally constructed for individual belief, and for the guidance of individual behavior. Individuals believed, and made their own individual responses. Bonhoeffer argues that Christian doctrines are about God's Lordship in Jesus Christ, they concern God's reign over the church and human society. Therefore, instead of seeking in them intent and meaning for individuals, their social intent and meaning for groups and institutions should be discovered. Words such as hope, acceptance, reconciliation, covenant, and the doctrines to which these words point have a social and institutional intent, and therefore call for a social and institutional response. These words, and others, speak of God's reign over the church and the world.

From this perspective, Christian doctrines are not seen as merely something to be believed, or rejected as unbelievable. Rather, they are seen as a guide for the reflection of leaders and members so that they may discern how God in Christ is Lord of the church and society. The appropriate response to God's work is not merely belief, but obedience in the church and community. Hope, acceptance, incarnation, and reconciliation denote Christian doctrines which have meaning for social-institutional life where God reigns, and where hope is created or destroyed, acceptance or rejection is experienced, reconciliation or alienation is supported and encouraged. God's work becomes flesh, incarnate, in those organizational arrangements where leaders and members have goals, use forms of power, cope with, adapt to, or ignore the community. In the creation of congregational and community life the social intent of Christian doctrine is expressed negatively or positively.

Leaders who are grasped by Christian faith reflect and act upon their understanding of the intention of God's reigning in the congregation and community. It can be disturbing and even threatening for church leaders and members finally to come to the conclusion that what is in the church is not good; that what is, and is powerful, lacks moral value and may be a living repudiation of Christian doctrine. The goals of a congregation, lacking in quality, filled with self-interest, using forms of power to maintain these unworthy goals, may, in fact, be a rejection of God's hope and acceptance for God's people.

This is the force of Bonhoeffer's idea. To examine the social intent of doctrine is to look piercingly at what is and to make discriminating judgments about conditions and events in the congregation and community. This means that where conditions exist such as manipulation by leaders, boredom of members, fearfulness of clergy, alienation and hostility of young confirmed members, these conditions must be exposed. Leaders must ask: Does God's reign mean this? Is the intent of Christian doctrines of hope, acceptance, and reconciliation to result in these conditions? Doing practical theology calls church members to look at actual conditions and the social intent of Christian doctrines most relevant to them, to see if there is congruency between the two. Leaders and members must not deceive themselves or others about what is *in* the church.

Authentic personhood, the second element from Bonhoeffer, is developed when leaders and members admit the true conditions that exist in a congregation, even when these violate personal commitments and concerns. Personal authenticity is always found in a "net of sociality," a social-institutional setting, not in individualistic isolation.[19] The wealth of material found in social-institutional settings must be faced forthrightly for persons to perceive themselves as authentic. Congregational life is one of the arenas where personhood and authenticity are at stake. Leadership and management of congregational life affect the personal authenticity of both leaders and members. The congregation is one important place where identity is formed. Personal awareness of the nature of congregational life and its impact on all participants is a first step toward authenticity. This means that "hostile information" is openly acknowledged. Information that differs from our own perceptions, goals, and values is information from others who see reality from a different perspective. It may or may not be accurate and true. Such information is essential for both leaders and members to establish personal authenticity.

Authenticity in the church calls for a second step, that of seeing the congregation, the "net of sociality" in which there is a common humanity. This is the location where God, the Beyond, the Other outside our grasp, is in the midst of human life.

Bonhoeffer states the case clearly: "What authority has Barth for saying that the other in himself is trivial and temporal (*Epistle to the Romans*, Eng. trans., p. 452), when this is the very man that God commands us to love? God has made our neighbor 'of supreme significance' in himself. The emissary of the unknown God; but he is of supreme significance in himself, because God considers him significant. Am I ultimately to be in the world alone with God?" "To be one with God and with one's neighbor is not something which I do for God. . . . The neighbor is not a sort of fool by means of which I practice the love of God." Authenticity is discovered and received in organizations in which individuals participate, but which also have their own unique, forming characteristics. Therefore, social structures and personal authenticity cannot be separated as though one can be authentic and discover authenticity only by oneself.[20] The way in which leaders and a congregation deal with members' personal goals and personal goals for the congregation, use various forms of power, and respond to information through persons from the environment establishes or violates authentic personhood for all, leaders and members. God's reign is affirmed or denied as congregational life is developed and personal authenticity is encouraged, created, or ignored.

The third element for doing practical theology is that the church—the community of Christians and fellowship of believers—is more than a collection of individuals. A major problem for

Bonhoeffer in *The Communion of Saints* is the relationship between individual being and social being. "Man's entire spirituality," he states, "is interwoven with sociality, and rests upon the basic relation of I and Thou."[21] Social existence, he maintains, was prior to individual existence. Social realities have a uniqueness and character (spirit) of their own that affect a person's spirit. This book, using categories of social and organizational theory not available to Bonhoeffer, has attempted to make this point as forcefully as possible. Social existence is the creation of persons who may or may not be reflective about their creation, who may or may not discern a relationship between Christian faith and their creations, who may or may not perceive that the church is the location of God's reign. Social existence in the church is in the form of congregations. Congregations are not mere collections of individuals. They have character, climate, purposes, forms of power, and relationships to the environment which have consequences for all members. They are, therefore, a legitimate object of reflection.

This means, practically, that leaders must be reflective about the conditions of congregational and community life; about their own assumptions, sentiments, habits, and values; and about how these have consequences for the spirits of persons as well as the spirit of the congregation. Truthfulness has its most profound consequences in organizational responses where the spirit of the congregation which affects the spirits of persons is transformed. Truthfulness about one's own sentiments, values, assumptions, and habits as a leader implies transformation in the nature and purposes of leadership. Truthfulness about the congregation implies transformation in congregational life.

Leaders and members cannot perceive the social intent of doctrine, or the formative effect of congregational life on authentic personhood, or see the congregation as more and other than a collection of individuals, without some hunches as to how to respond to God's reign in the church. This suggests the final element which is important from Bonhoeffer. God's reign, God's transcendence in human life, is a social/ethical reality, not a theory. God reigns in the most concrete realities of life, or God does not reign. Christianity is not just a matter of individuals knowing doctrine, Bible, and church history, although these are resources for faithful living. Christianity is experiencing life in which God is Lord in Jesus Christ. God's hope, acceptance, and reconciliation are realities we can experience. They are not merely doctrines to be believed. God's active presence is among people as they exhibit hope, acceptance, and reconciliation. John Calvin made this point in another way: "Preaching is to no avail, except the gospel be in the Church."

Congregational life as the social/ethical reality bearing witness to the reign of God requires love and justice. Justice and love look different from different perspectives. To persons who have personal goals and personal goals for the congregation yet unachieved, and who perceive that the forms of power are being used to thwart them, love and justice remain rhetorical. This perception will continue until those who use forms of power make explicit the values or theological commitment which have guided them in the creation of congregational life. When they do so the ground for such judgments can be publicly examined, and even disputed. A social/ethical community requires processes where the ethics and theological commitments can be confirmed or modified or denied by those who are part of the society.

This chapter is not *a* theology for congregational life. It is intended to provide categories of thought which may be helpful to members of a congregation. Within Christendom we think historically and culturally from different traditional doctrines. Lutherans think from a doctrine of justification by faith in which God's acceptance is a central aspect of Christian faith. Christians of the Presbyterian Reformed tradition have traditionally emphasized God's reign over all of creation. More recently, God's reconciling work in the church and society has been lifted up confessionally by the United Presbyterian Church. In an earlier book, *Change in the Church: A Source of Hope* (Westminster Press, 1971, see especially Ch. 5), I intentionally thought and wrote from this confessional stance. Still other denominations have identified the covenant between God and persons as the key perspective on Christian faith for themselves.

All these doctrines have social intent. All need to find their expression in concrete forms of the church and society. All have consequences in action. The social intent and actions to implement the intent have meaning for the "net of sociality" in which the identity of persons is being formed. In the church where authentic personhood may be formed and found, the community of persons called a congregation, with its unique spirit, has consequences for the neighbor. Relation with the neighbor in church and society is characterized by love and justice, so that congregational life is first and foremost an expression of Christian faith, a social/ethical reality that demonstrates God's reign.

The role of leaders has been mentioned because they have special responsibility to understand their activity as an exercise in practical theology which has social/ethical consequences. Many leaders already know this. They are thinking and acting theologically. But much of this thought and action is unintentional and inconsistent. The personal authenticity of leaders and public exposure of their actions and the basis for those actions are needed to demonstrate the social intention of doctrine, as it is expressed in the social/ethical reality of the church in its day-by-day existence. Categories of thinking and acting that relate to what persons in the church experience are needed. Handles must be provided. Most traditions have doctrines from which to work, if leadership is provided in doing practical theology.

CHAPTER 7

Getting On with Ministry in the Church

This book has been written with two basic assumptions. First, what has been traditionally called administration, its theory and practice in the church, is a human creation. It is therefore limited in scope and adequacy for the church in any particular moment. The second is that at this moment administration is a central problem for professionals, lay leaders, and members of congregations.

The past generation of professionals frequently looked with disdain at administration and administrative practices. The "real work" of ministry was found in preaching and pastoral care of individuals. The laity acquiesced to this view and perpetuated it. Without attention to administration, congregations have been allowed to drift without direction. Year after year governing boards were found doing many of the same things in the same style, until programs died from apathy and lack of support and membership dwindled. Ministers have attempted to preach charismatically to give congregations direction. Governing boards have been stacked by nominating committees under the minister's influence to provide the "right" leaders to move a congregation. Clergy have spent all the "relationship capital" developed over years of pastoral care and counseling in attempts to mobilize the members, either to move the church in new directions or to maintain the status quo in the face of rising challenges. There has been administration, even by those who scoff at the activity.

The phrase "wise rule" was used earlier in this book to denote activities different in kind from those normally associated with administration. The late H. Richard Niebuhr and Kenneth Underwood, and more recently James Gustafson, have used the phrase to resurrect a major understanding of Christ's ministry which developed in the Reformed tradition with roots in the writings of John Calvin.

Calvin described the office (function) that was assigned Christ in his ministry as having three parts: prophetic, priestly, and kingly. Calvin maintained that these three activities were necessary for our knowledge of God's work in Christ and for receiving the benefits of this work. It is important to emphasize that prophetic, priestly, and kingly activities were *all* essential in the witness, the sharing, and the expression of God's work in Christ, and in caring for God's people. Wise rule has been used as a contemporary way to refer to the ministry of Christ the King, caring for his people. Ministers and congregational members do not normally think of administration as an activity for carrying out Christ's ministry, but wise rule is Christ's ministry, and, therefore, the ministry of both clergy and laity.

It is strangely characteristic of Protestantism that the prophetic-preaching and sacramental-pastoral roles have been emphasized while the kingly, governance, or wise-rule activity has been largely neglected. Most legitimization is given to particular kinds of sacramental-priestly and pastoral functions. Perhaps to a lesser degree, we legitimize prophetic-preaching functions. But in Protestantism there is little understanding and legitimization of kingly-governance or political leadership activities. Much stress within church organizations is related to the conflict between the priorities assigned to these different ministerial functions. A great deal of stress is also created by those who use a political style rooted in the feudal tradition. Such persons see congregations, judicatories, or church agencies as fiefdoms to be ruled autocratically; as an empire governed from the top down by an elitist, minority group; or as a political state, in which those in power determine the objectives and control the allocation and use of resources.

We encourage abuses of power and inefficiency when we think of the ministry of Christ primarily in terms of what the minister does. The functions characteristic of Christ's ministry have been ascribed not to the church, Christ's people who must do his ministry, but to the clergy, one group of Christ's people. It ought to be no surprise that this one group finds itself incapable of performing with any adequacy and effectiveness the total ministry of Christ.

This book suggests that the problem of understanding the membership in the church and ministry by clergy and laity is related to the turbulence in congregations. We must now focus on the organizations and the methods of governance in these organizations as at least a partial answer to this problem. There is a theological as well as an organizational basis for this focus. Calvin saw *three* activities as necessary and essential expressions of God's work in Christ. All three belong together, expressing their own aspect of that work in unity with one another. It is possible for the three activities to contradict each other. When that happens, the lack of a unified understanding of Christ's ministry and its implications for *our* ministry has both theological and practical consequences both for persons in the church and for the church organization. Wise rule is one of those essential activities, along with prophetic and priestly activities, which helps shape the witness of Christ's people to God's work among them. It is in itself a witness to that work. Governance is an activity that is practical, concrete, and a profound expression of theological reflection.

There is a wholeness to Christ's ministry which is not found normally in the church today. Congregations expect that the minister will "do it"—whatever the ministry is. Cultural conditioning, theological education, and personal style and proclivities have combined to produce both ministers and laypersons with expectations which are theologically heretical. They envision a truncated ministry of Christ, done by professionals. In the meantime, the church languishes. Leaders quit or are dismissed. Structures are reorganized. New coalitions vote out the "rascals who produced the latest mess." The resources, energy, imagination, and life of members are sapped in efforts that are not the ministry of Christ's people.

Getting hold of self and ministry means getting hold of that which shapes the church as an institution. Many books and articles have been written on the crises of the clergy. Dozens of studies have been made. The sobering fact is that one cannot discuss the problems of the clergy without discussing the problems of the laity, and the context of both, the church as an institution. Both clergy and laity have identity problems in the church today. The dilemmas of one group cannot be discussed intelligently without examining what is happening to the other. If a minister has problems of role image, authority, power, function, and expectations, it is because the laity is in motion. The context within which both are defined, the institutional church, is ambiguous, turbulent, and in a state of redefinition. The study of one group, clergy, yields poor and indirect information about the second group, laity, and almost no information about the church, which institutionalizes roles, expectations, images, and patterns of authority.

A unilateral definition of appropriate roles and behaviors for ministers is hardly relevant to institutional reality. An institutional answer is needed to an institutional problem. Both clergy and laity must define ministry together, and develop the appropriate institutional responses. Laypersons need to come to terms with both their ministry and the clergy's before congregational life and ministry can become vital and purposeful.

These elements for reflection about ministry are not new; they have had their influence in every age of the church. Christians in each historical era have had some understanding of the "essence" of the church according to particular Scriptural and historical norms. (See Figure 7 for a scheme that identifies the various elements and their relations to each other.)

An understanding of the "essence" of the church is expressed in particular images that have consequences for defining roles and functions of both clergy and laity. The environment has its impact in calling forth responses that are more or less appropriate to meet the challenges. The images of the church and roles and functions of the clergy provide an institutional means for responding to environmental threats or challenges.

Hans Küng has documented the development of the different images of the church in changing environments.[22] Dominant images that have characterized the church at particular moments have been:

1. A persecuted people in a hostile, pagan world.
2. A community committed to building up the faith and morality of its members.
3. An institution mobilized for a frontal assault on heresy. It sees itself primarily as the protector and embodier of truth.
4. A strong clergy-dominated institution that engages in battles and victories, rewards and punishments in order that it can impose particular dogmatic formulas.
5. A school for truth and a strong community of learners.
6. A religious culture community with a powerful set of symbols and with saving power in sacred images.
7. A well-ordered, disciplined community with laws, binding rituals, and norms for daily life.
8. A priesthood of all believers characterized by an educated, knowing, distinct clergy and an uneducated, ignorant mass of believers. A dominant teaching office in contrast to powerless, uneducated laity.

FIGURE 7

RELATIONSHIP AFFECTING THE THEORY
AND PRACTICE OF MINISTRY

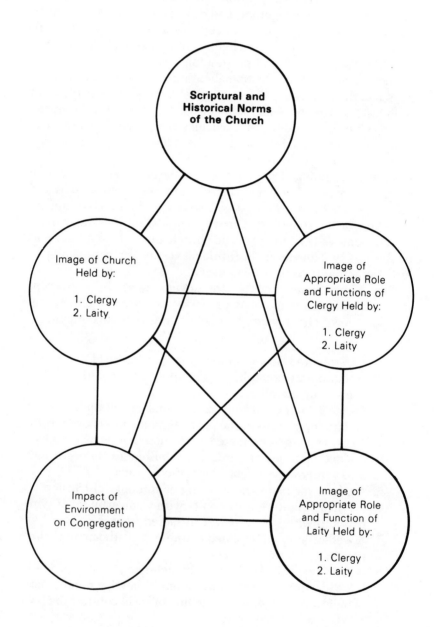

9. The mystical body of Christ. The church as a mystical community.
10. People of God, brought together in love and the Holy Spirit. Clergy and other church officers are subservient to the people.

Each dominant image implies characteristic assumptions, habits, and activities by both clergy and laity. But a reality of church life is that a mixture of images exists. There is no single dominant image, but competing and conflicting images with their concomitant implied definitions of what it means to be clergy and laity.

Images and theologies that support the appropriateness of particular images are conveyed by the church as an organization. In congregational life, as organization, one sees the power of images and theologies expressed in structure, goals, political processes, polity, and roles and functions of clergy and laity. Organization is the mediator of what persons believe to be the "essence" of Christian faith. Strengths, life-styles, sentiments, and habits of clergy and laity affect and are affected by the mediating organization. Congregations today show the influence of past dominant images, past roles and functions of clergy and laity, past environments, and the peculiar personal characteristics of clergy and laity in those past organizations. Confusion and lack of certainty of images, and the accompanying organizational characteristics, create identity problems for both laity and clergy.

Reformation of the church has always begun with clarity and certainty about a set of images for church, clergy, and laity— images with their roots in an interpretation of Scriptural and historical norms, images that can be a responsive expression of Christian faith in a changed environment. Each age, as Küng has stated, has its own image of the church and the accompanying images for clergy and laity, arising out of particular historical situations.

The challenge for our time is to create those forms of the church and its ministry which are expressive of Christian faith in a changing world. Clarity and certainty about the nature and character of the church, and hence, too, about roles and function appropriate for clergy and laity, are more difficult to grasp in a time of turbulence. The easiest alternatives are, actively or passively, to encourage the clergy to minister in a very limited sense—to do pastoral counseling, to call on the sick, elderly, and distressed—or to stress the ritualistic sacramental functions of worship. Both alternatives imply a passive laity—a theological and practical impossibility. A significant segment of laity will not tolerate a passive role in the light of the claims of Christian faith on them.

Most clearly stated, the clergy's identity crisis is actually an identity crisis of the laity as well. This is due not to role confusion, as some would suggest, but to a lack of certainty as to what the church is about in a changing society. When the purposes of a congregation, not the universal church, are clear and certain within this small world, the minister and members together will be able to discern what they are both to do together, to take full advantage of their special training, resources, interests, and commitments. Reformation, renewal, and revitalization of the church have begun in each instance, not in theological seminaries or at the instigation of the central authority, but in particular congregations. The reformulation of roles and functions for clergy and laity will be done in congregations where theology and the practice of ministry are brought together to focus on the wholeness of congregational life, not just on preaching, teaching, pastoral care, and counseling. The effort must be made to use the resources of clergy and laity in their uniqueness, to create a congregation which in its entirety is expressive of God's Lordship in Jesus Christ. An underlying and fundamental concept of Christian faith is a value: wholeness, at-oneness, the need for a whole people of God with one story to fit unreconciled pieces together, to provide a living reality that brings at-oneness to human life. The appropriate relationship between theology and the practice of ministry results in activity that creates community. The mediator between Christian doctrine which has social intent and the practice of ministry is the life of a congregation.

Practical theology, the thinking through of the social intent of Christian doctrine, is to enable congregations to establish, in theory and practice, the conditions for their own existence. We learn from doing this that the church has implications for all of society.

An image of the church that lies behind the writing of this book is that of a moral community. First and foremost it is aware of and concerned about the morality of congregational life. James Gustafson, in *The Church as Moral Decision-Maker,* has emphasized the church's role in society. His key phrase in discussing the church is "community of moral discourse," by which he means "a gathering of people with the explicit intention to survey and critically discuss their personal and social responsibility in the light of moral convictions about which there is some conviction and to which there is some loyalty."[23]

The position advocated in this book is more limited in scope than Gustafson's. The situation and material for reflection is provided by the congregation. While I am in great sympathy with his advocacy of moral discourse about world issues, the sophistication and knowledge required for intelligent, authentic discussion is simply not available to most congregations. Neither clergy nor laity is prepared for such responsible talking. This lack, however, does not negate the need for responsible moral reflection upon the material at hand, namely, the conditions of congregational life and the relation of the congregation to its community.

If leaders and members cannot examine, criticize, evaluate, and test the conditions of congregational life created by them as they have attempted to express their theological commitments in the practice of ministry, then it is futile for anyone to talk of moral discourse about larger and more distant realities. The material for reflection is in the social intent of doctrines already believed, the information provided by the personal goals, structure, political processes, rules and procedures in the congregation, and from members who have a variety of experiences with the community surrounding the congregation.

WISE RULE IN THE CHURCH

For truly wise rule a vision is needed of a larger "public," a congregation and a community whose interests and needs transcend those of its contending groups and vocal partisans. Rule in the church needs to be set within the framework of a common humanity. All members have a common humanity in the church. All are part of an institution that has in one way or another dealt with their personal goals and personal goals for the congregation, and consequently has touched them in those areas of fundamental loyalties and commitments. Clergy and laity all live with limits. They need reflection and truthfulness about the conditions of this common humanity and the limits that constrain professional and nonprofessional church members.

This book is written for church leaders because there is a great amount of partisanship among church leaders today. There is need, not for one-sided or partisan leadership groups, but for leaders who have a sense of common humanity and a commitment to truthfulness.

Hans Küng, in *Truthfulness: The Future of the Church*, states: "In this way, also for the modern world, truth is bound to man's personal existence—that is, to his truthfulness. Veracity is the *conditio sine qua non* of truth. Only in truthfulness is the truth of a person revealed. Only the honest man is disposed to apprehend the truth which sustains him. The truth is closed to those who are dishonest with themselves. In this sense truthfulness is much more basic than truth itself. Even those who cannot agree on truth must nevertheless agree on truthfulness. Honesty makes dialogue possible. For those living in a pluralistic society, it is not truth but honesty, truthfulness, which is the basis of all tolerance and of all social life and cooperation. Thus does honesty become a basic ethical demand, touching everyone and everything concerning man's relationship to himself, to society and to God."[24]

The sense of common humanity and the commitment to truthfulness is not only fundamental to Christian faith but is also practically necessary in times of confusion about identity. What it means to be clergy or laity may be answered by retreating to the roles, models, and assumptions of a limited past experience.

"Men can abandon any attempt at personal experiment out of the conviction that they already know what any experiment with their own lives will lead to. For making things coherent means imagining they are known and understood by the simple act of an individual's will. Thus the principle of security and regularity comes to be enshrined through the willful illusion that the young person, or the older person who carries the scar from his youth, has somehow already tested all possibilities open to him."[25] Richard Sennett in this statement has described the condition whereby persons in times of identity crises attempt to purify experience so that the contradictions and ambiguities in the surrounding social world are eliminated. Elimination is accomplished through maintenance or establishment of satisfying organizational goals in worship, preaching, and congregational life through use of the forms of power. The partisanship or one-sidedness which is seen in the church may be symptomatic of that desire for purity, for a noncontradictory experience which Sennett has described as an illness. One way of dealing with a crisis of identity is to seek to control, reduce, or eliminate everything in one's social world which suggests an alternative style of behavior, idea, assumption, sentiment, or goal.

A more satisfactory way of dealing with identity crises is to increase one's participation so that the common bonds necessary in times of uncertainty and ambiguity grow out of common experiences of reflection and participation in ministry. Integrity, dignity, and personal authenticity are discovered and received in those moments of truthfulness where common bonds develop during common experiences. Common bonds allow for deviation and innovation, and for freedom to develop new roles and functions for clergy and laity. New goals, structural forms, political processes, and polity—in other words, a new common humanity can develop when common bonds exist. Common bonds do not imply sameness, but suggest the glue that binds persons together so that experimentation can take place in meeting the challenges of a puzzling social world.

Wise rule is built on a reflective model. Persons who are not sure who they are can discover new possibilities for themselves, for others, and for the church and its ministry as they look at social realities and think together about their own Christian commitments and how these may be best expressed in congregational and community life. New institutional forms can be created under conditions that reduce tensions and defensiveness sufficiently so that persons are free to explore alternatives.

There are three important characteristics of leaders who desire to rule wisely and well today. First, they must bring together in themselves theology and the practice of ministry. They will require substantive reflection on how to achieve this integration. They must ask: How shall we understand the congregation and the community? How shall we understand the congregation with persons and groups whose goals are in competition and conflict, and which vary in quality? How can we enable the congregation to reflect on the quality of its goals, and which goals should have highest priority? What processes are needed to enable the congregation to inquire about the care of its members, and its care of the surrounding community?

Leaders are needed who can participate in reflection and lead the congregation in reflection. Elitist leaders who are recognized solely for their status in the community, or for the size of their financial contribution to the congregation, may not have the quality of thought needed by turbulent congregations. Leaders are needed who have an awareness of their own strengths, values, and knowledge, and who recognize that their knowledge is historically conditioned and partial. Knowledge for adequate reflection goes beyond personal values and limited perspective. Personal authenticity in leadership requires an awareness of self and of how personal style, strengths, and knowledge intersect with one's goals and commitments and, consequently, how they affect those who have a common humanity in the congregation.

A major problem in leadership occurs when reflection breaks down, when the glue based upon common experience no longer binds persons together. For then truthfulness is threatened. When leadership groups are threatened, when they are composed of only one type of person with special interests, the demands of truthfulness are difficult to meet. Shallowness, evasiveness, and defensiveness result from challenges. Diversity among leaders must be developed and maintained through political processes so that persons with different styles, strengths, values, knowledge, and experiences work toward a common humanity, and model among themselves some alternatives for the congregation. With such diversity, information from different parts of the congregation and different aspects of church-community life can flow to leadership groups with ease, and become part of the mixture of information, personal characteristics, and theological sources that are necessary for reflection.

Information that matters most to members of the congregation is not gleaned through questionnaires and surveys. Knowledge of a congregation's life and relationships to a community is constructed, developed, and maintained in the experiences of members. Their involvements, labors, relationships, speech, and reflection are the material for further reflection, criticism, and reformation. Truthfulness and personal authenticity begin with conditions as they are perceived by members of a congregation. Congregational truthfulness and authenticity exist when a congregation recognizes that all members do not see the congregation or the congregation's relation to community from the same set of Christian commitments, values, experiences.

An important characteristic for leaders is reflection. Leaders need to understand how persons act to construct congregational patterns which inhibit or thwart expression of the social intent of Christian doctrine. Theological reflection is needed on information about congregational life. Further reading and discussion of "basic Christian beliefs," valuable as it may be, is not enough. Reflection is needed that will confront persons with their own creations, their mundaneness, inequities, their ties to economic and political interests. A primary requisite for leaders and leadership groups is truthfulness about such information, about the way we deal with it even when we do not like it, and when it opposes our own interests and perceptions. Truthfulness does not demand that we give up our own perceptions, but that we examine them, and be open to correction through new information. Truthfulness is a sign of personal authenticity and organizational integrity. The conditions in congregational life that inhibit or ignore truthfulness must be exposed, criticized, and transformed.

Reflection about concrete congregational life is needed if theology and the practice of ministry are to be brought together so that each increases in quality and depth. The first level of reflection is among leaders and leadership groups. The second level is among members of the congregation who need to receive information and interpret its meaning with leaders. They, too, need to reflect about the social intent of their Christian beliefs in relation to events and conditions in congregational life and the community. A common bond and a common sense of humanity needs to be developed among members, and between leaders and members. This can take place only through reflection on significant information and through common experiences. Otherwise the lack of a sense of common humanity with some shared purposes and directions prevents leaders from making meaningful decisions about congregational life. Leaders often vote, and in the process of voting think they are making decisions. But little of significance is implemented if a common bond between leaders and members is not there.

Much self-deception still exists among leaders, particularly clergy, who perceive that leadership is handing down pronouncements, decisions, and comments in a unilateral, authoritative manner. Leadership is a function of the people, as much as it is of leaders. Strong, educated, resourceful people do not tolerate unilateral, authoritative leadership. Passive, dependent, undereducated persons tolerate so-called "strong leadership." Conditions no longer exist that made possible the "high doctrine of the ministry" developed in feudal society. And that style will not solve the identity crisis for either clergy or laity. The model of clergy and lay leaders as reflective persons each with integrity in knowledge and function is more viable for our time. A role for clergy in teaching, assisting, equipping, organizing, supporting, and enabling leaders and members points to a higher doctrine of ministry, and one that is needed for both church and world.

Another characteristic important for leaders is the ability to design the processes for ruling wisely and well. Human processes for gathering information from members, for assisting the congregation in establishing its relation to its community, for activating and mobilizing members and their resources, for reflecting about the intent of Christian beliefs in relation to the realities which they experience are essential. In a separate forthcoming volume, descriptions of processes for activating members of congregations will be provided.

A third characteristic important for leaders is the commitment to enable the congregation to generate a vision for itself which is helpful to its members and the community. Leaders cannot impose a vision. They can initiate the processes and participate actively to contribute to the vision. They can also offer criteria by which the congregation can make discerning judgments about the quality of its vision. Congregations languish for lack of a worthwhile vision.

Leaders are generators of vision among God's people, and they hold certain criteria as a mirror before God's people to enable them to make judgments about the quality and adequacy of their vision. Criteria that may serve as a basis for reflection and development are:

1. A hopeful vision for the whole congregation that brings at-oneness to congregational life, and which serves to guide, direct, and judge human efforts toward that end.
2. A vision that invites and claims active, rather than passive, members.
3. A vision that is for others, extending to the community as well as toward more humane, loving care of congregational members.
4. A vision that has two sides, holding both promise of a concrete future which is more expressive of Christian faith, and a judgment on the inadequacy of the present. The vision should be a powerful reminder that in spite of human claims, the Kingdom of God is not yet fully manifest among us.
5. A vision in which freedom, personal responsibility, and creativity are found within the framework of congregational life, not outside. Freedom, personal responsibility, and creativity are found within the limits of institutional life, not in an anarchy of rampant individualism.
6. A vision that holds the possibility that the intent of fundamental Christian beliefs and doctrines should find their more concrete form in social life, human relations, and the institutional forms of life, including the church.

NOTES

1. Duncan Shaw, *The General Assemblies of the Church of Scotland 1560–1600* (Edinburgh: St. Andrew Press, 1964). An excellent documentation of the struggle of early reformers in adapting and transforming the feudal legacy is contained in this study.

2. James Luther Adams, *On Being Human Religiously* (Beacon Press, 1976), p. 134.

3. Richard Sennett, *The Uses of Disorder: Personal Identity and City Life* (Middlesex, England: Penguin Books, 1973).

4. Erich Fromm, *The Anatomy of Human Destructiveness* (Holt, Rinehart & Winston, 1973), pp. 7–8.

5. Ibid., pp. 8–9.

6. Amitai Etzioni, *A Comparative Analysis of Complex Organizations: On Power, Involvement, and Their Correlates* (Free Press of Glencoe, 1961). The major themes and ideas of this book have influenced my own thought greatly, as anyone who has read this book will appreciate. I have used a different starting point in developing a perspective. Etzioni is interested in compliance, power, and involvement. I have begun with human passions expressed in goals and then related them to many of the organizational correlates that Etzioni has suggested. Church persons have sources in theology, transcendent elements, historical experiences in the church, and the relationship of Christianity to a sense of self which feeds passions, which are expressed in goals. The emphasis on power and involvement that Etzioni has made is appropriate for the church. I have borrowed heavily from him on this point but have attempted to relate power and involvement to goals and ultimately to human passions. See particularly Part II, "Compliance, Goals and Effectiveness," for a description of his theory. An excellent corrective to Etzioni's emphasis on compliance can be found in Charles Perrow, *Organizational Analysis: A Sociological View* (Prentice-Hall, 1965).

7. William A. Gamson, *Power and Discontent* (Dorsey Press, 1968).

8. Amitai Etzioni has explained the variety of responses to the use of and response to different kinds of power. See *A Comparative Analysis of Complex Organizations*, pp. 3–22.

9. Lewis Mumford, *The Pentagon of Power*, Vol. II of *The Myth of the Machine* (Harcourt Brace Jovanovich, 1970). See Ch. 2, "The Return of the Sun God."

10. Edward A. Tiryakian, "Structural Sociology," in *Theoretical Sociology: Perspectives and Developments*, ed. John C. McKinney and Edward A. Tiryakian (Appleton-Century-Crofts, 1970), p. 115.

11. Keith R. Bridston, *Church Politics* (World Publishing Co., 1969).

12. Alan Richardson, *The Political Christ* (Westminster Press, 1973).

13. See C. Wright Mills, *The Power Elite* (Oxford University Press, 1956), for a description of the structuralist perspective. Robert A. Dahl, in *Preface to Democratic Theory* (University of Chicago Press, 1965), provides a contemporary description of the pluralist theory.

14. See Amitai Etzioni, "Toward a Macrosociology," in *Theoretical Sociology: Perspectives and Developments*, ed. McKinney and Tiryakian, pp. 72–81. In this essay Etzioni is developing a theory of social change which is based upon a cybernetic model of guided change which includes decision-making centers and a communication network.

15. William R. Dill, "The Impact of Environment on Organizational Development," in *Readings in Organization Theory: Open-System Approaches*, ed. John G. Maurer (Random House, 1971), p. 84.

16. Howard S. Becker and Blanche Geer, "Latent Culture: A Note on the Theory of Latent Social Roles," in *Readings in Organization Theory*, ed. Mauer, pp. 270–277.

17. Karl Rahner, *Theological Investigations: Confrontations*, Vol. II (London: Darton, Longman & Todd, 1974), pp. 118–119.

18. Jürgen Moltmann, "The Lordship of Christ and Human Society," in Jürgen Moltmann and Jürgen Weissbach, *Two Studies in the Theology of Bonhoeffer*, tr. Reginald H. and Ilse Fuller (Charles Scribner's Sons, 1967), pp. 21–94.

19. Dietrich Bonhoeffer, *The Communion of Saints: A Dogmatic Inquiry Into the Sociology of the Church*, tr. Ronald Gregor Smith (Harper & Row, 1961), p. 227.

20. Ibid., pp. 50–52.

21. Ibid., p. 48.

22. Hans Küng, *The Church* (Sheed & Ward, 1968), pp. 6–14.

23. James M. Gustafson, *The Church as Moral Decision-Maker* (Pilgrim Press, 1970), p. 84.

24. Hans Küng, *Truthfulness: The Future of the Church* (Sheed & Ward, 1968), p. 41.

25. Sennett, *The Uses of Disorder*, p. 30.